SHAGGYCOAT

The Biography of a Beaver by CLARENCE HAWKES

Author of Black Bruin, The Biography of a Bear

Shovelhorns, The Biography of a Moose, etc.

PHILADELPHIA MACRAE SMITH COMPANY PUBLISHERS

Dedicated to my Little Brother, the Venetian, who, living in a house that his hands have made, surrounded by a moat of his own device, the head of a large family and a citizen in a goodly community, is more like man in his mode of life, than any other of God's creatures.

* * * * *

KING OF ALL THE BEAVERS

Till he came unto a streamlet In the middle of the forest, To a streamlet still and tranquil, That had overflowed its margin, To a dam made by the beavers, To a pond of quiet water, Where knee-deep the trees were standing, Where the water-lilies floated, Where the rushes waved and whispered. On the dam stood Pau-Puk-Keewis, On the dam of trunks and branches, Through whose chinks the water spouted, O'er whose summit flowed the streamlet. From the bottom rose the beaver, Looked with two great eyes of wonder, Eyes that seemed to ask a question, At the stranger Pau-Puk-Keewis.

--LONGFELLOW.

* * * * *

CONTENTS

A FOURFOOTED AMERICAN

INTRODUCTORY

Just how long the red man, in company with his wild brothers, the deer, the bear, the wolf, the buffalo, and the beaver had inhabited the continent of North America, before the white man came, is a problem for speculation; but judging from all signs it was a very long time. The Mound Builders of Ohio and the temple builders of Mexico speak to us out of a dim prehistoric past, but the song and story of the red man and many a quaint Indian tradition tell us how he lived, and something of his life and religion.

If we look carefully into these quaint tales and folk-lore of the red man, we shall find that he lived upon very intimate relations with all his wild brothers and while he hunted them for meat and used their skins for garments and their hides for bowstrings, yet he knew and understood them and treated them with a reverence that his white brother has never been able to feel.

Before the red man bent the bow he sought pardon from the deer or bear for the act that he was about to commit. Often when he had slain the wild creature, he made offerings to its departed spirit, and also wore its likeness tattooed upon his skin as a totem. Thus we see that these denizens of the wilderness were creatures of importance, playing their part in the life of the red man, even before the white man came to these shores. But that they should have continued to play a prominent part after the advent of the white man is still more vital to us.

It was principally for beaver skins that the Hudson Bay Company unfurled its ensign over the wilds of Labrador and upon the bleak shores of Hudson Bay, during the seventeenth century. H. B. C. was the monogram upon their flag. Their coat of arms had a beaver in each quarter of the shield, and their motto was Pro Pelle Cutem, meaning skin for skin. An official of the company once interpreted the H. B. C. as "here before Christ," saying that the company was ahead of the missionaries with its emblem of civilization.

For more than two hundred and twenty-five years this company has held sway over a country larger than all the kingdoms of Europe, counting out Russia. For the first one hundred years it was the only government and held power of life and death over all living in its jurisdiction.

It was because the Indian knew that he could get so many knives or so much cloth for a beaver skin, that he endured the terrible cold of the Arctic winter, and hunted and trapped close to the sweep of the Arctic Circle. For this valuable skin white trappers built their camp-fire and slept upon ten feet of snow. It was a common day's work for a trapper to drag his snow-shoes over twenty miles of frozen waste to visit his traps.

For the pelts of the beaver, otter and mink, those bloody battles were fought between the Hudson Bay Company men and the trappers of the Northwest Company. The right to trap in disputed territory was held by the rifle, and human life was not worth one beaver skin.

In those old days, so full of hardship and peril, the beaver skin was the standard of value in all the Hudson Bay Company's transactions. Ten muskrat skins, or two mink skins made a beaver skin, and the beaver skin bought the trapper his food and blanket.

The first year of its existence the Hudson Bay Company paid seventy-five per cent. upon all its investments, and for over two centuries it has been rolling up wealth, while to-day it is pushing further and further north and is more prosperous than ever, and all this at the expense of the beaver and his warm-coated fellows.

Even the civilization of Manhattan comprising what is now New York and Brooklyn was founded upon the beaver skin. It was a common thing in the days of Wouter Van Twiller, for the colony of the Hudson to send home to the Netherlands eighty thousand beaver skins a year.

John Jacob Astor, the head of the rich New York family laid the foundations for his colossal wealth in beaver skins, and this is the history of the frontier in nearly all parts of the country.

But there were other ways in which the beaver was advancing the white man's civilization and making his pathway smooth, even before he came to destroy his four-footed friend, for the beaver was the first woodsman to fell the forest and clear broad acres of land that were afterward used for tillage. He also was the first engineer to dam the streams and rivers. To-day almost anywhere in New England you can see traces of his industry. You may not recognize it, but it is there.

Nearly all the small meadows along our streams were made by the beavers and acres of the best tillage that New England contains were cleared by them.

They dammed the stream to protect their communities from their enemies, and flowed large sections of territory. All the timber upon the flooded district soon rotted and fell into the lake and in this way great sections were cleared.

Each spring the freshets brought down mud and deposited it in the bottom of the lake until it was rich with rotting vegetable matter and decaying wood. Then the trapper came and caught the beaver, so that the dam fell into disuse. Finally it was swept away entirely, and a broad fertile meadow was left where there had been a woodland lake. Thus the beaver has made meadowland for us all the way from the Atlantic to the Pacific, and we have shoved him further and further from his native haunts.

To-day he has entirely disappeared from New England, with the exception of a few scattered colonies in Maine, where he is protected by his neighbors who have become interested in his ways. There is also a protected colony in Northern New York, and a few scattered beavers in the mountains of Virginia, but this industrious prehistoric American has largely disappeared from the United States, east of the Rocky Mountains. His home, if he now has any in the land he once possessed, is in Montana, where he lives in something of his old abandon. There he still makes new meadow lands for the cattle men and rears his conical house in his forest lake.

Like the red man he has been thrust further and further into the wild; retreating before the shriek of the locomotive, and those ever advancing steel rails. But the debt that we owe the beaver will remain as long as we cut grass upon our meadow land, or appropriate the coat of this sleek American for our own.

Thus the blazed trail is pushed on and on into the wilderness and the old is succeeded by the new. Animals, birds, and trees disappear, and brick blocks and telephone poles take their places.

Though he will ultimately disappear from the continent, we shall always be heavily in debt to the beaver for the important part that he played in the colonial history of America.

Like the red man he is a true American, for he was here before Columbus, and his pelt was the prize for which the wilderness was scoured. His only disqualification for citizenship in our great and growing country is that he is a four-footed American, while we, his masters, are bipeds.

CHAPTER I

FUGITIVES

At the time when our story begins, Shaggycoat was a two-year-old beaver, fleeing with his grandfather from he knew not what. They had been so happy in the woodland lake, which was their home before the terrible intrusion, that the whole matter seemed more like a hideous dream than a reality.

When Shaggycoat thought of the old days and his family, he could remember warm summer afternoons upon clean sand banks, where he and his brothers and sisters frolicked together. Then there were such delightful swims in the deep lake, where they played water-tag, and all sorts of games, diving and plunging and swimming straight away, not to mention deep plunges to the bottom of the lake where they vied with one another in staying down. Then when they were hungry, the bulbs of the lily and a cluster of wild hops made a dinner that would make a beaver's mouth water; with perhaps some spicy bark added as a relish.

Then came the cold and the pond was covered with ice. They could still see the sun by day and the stars by night, but they could not come to the surface to breathe as they had done before. There were a great many air holes, and places under the ice where the water did not reach it, but for breathing space they had to depend largely upon the queer conical houses in which they lived and their burrows along the bank.

There was still another way to breathe that I had nearly forgotten. A beaver or any of these little Water Folks can come up to the surface and breathe against the ice. A big flat bubble is at once formed and as it strikes the ice it is purified and then the beaver breathes it in again and it is almost as fresh as though it came from the upper air. This he can do three or four times before having to find an air hole or going into one of the houses or burrows.

The beavers were very snug under the ice which kept away the wind and cold, and also their worst enemy, man.

The breath of the family made the houses warm, and as the walls were frozen solid, and were two or three feet thick, they were very hard to break into.

A store of wood had been laid up from which the bark was stripped for food as fast as it was needed, so that Beaver City had been very snug and comfortable, before the trouble came.

Then when they were sleeping through the short winter days, and prowling about the lake in the night in search of fresh twigs or sticks that had been frozen into the ice, the trouble began.

First there came the sound of pounding and soon there were holes in the ice near their supply of wood. Then occasionally a beaver who was hungry and had gone for breakfast was missed from the family or lodge where he lived. At first they thought he had gone for a swim on the lake and would soon come back, but when several had gone out to the winter's store and had not returned, the truth dawned upon some of the older and wiser beavers. Their forest lake had been invaded by some enemy, probably man, and one by one the colony was being slaughtered.

There is but one thing to do at such a time and that is to take safety in flight, for the beaver does not consider that he can match his cunning against that of man.

While the beavers were still considering whether to go at once or wait another day, there were sounds of heavy blows upon the tops of their houses and then there was a loud explosion and the water began to fall. Then they fled in every direction, some taking refuge in the burrows that they had dug under the banks all along the lake for such an emergency, while others sought to leave the lake altogether; some going up stream and some down. But the destruction of Beaver City had been planned very carefully by their cunning enemy, man, and most of them perished while leaving the lake.

When the men who were watching on the ice above saw a beaver swimming in the water under them, they would follow upon the ice, going just where the beaver went. The beaver would stay near the bottom of the lake as long as he could hold his breath, but finally he would have to come to the surface for air when the trapper would strike a hard blow upon the ice, stunning him, or perhaps killing him outright. Then he would cut a hole in the ice and fish out his unfortunate victim.

It was from such perils as these, although they were not fully understood by the beavers, that Shaggycoat and his grandfather fled the second night of this reign of terror. They would gladly have gone in a larger company, with Shaggycoat's brothers and sisters and with his father and mother, but all the rest of their immediate family were missing and they never saw them again.

They went in the inky night, before the moon had risen. Silently, like dark shadows, they glided along the bottom of the lake, which was still about half full of water, for the white man's thunder had not been able to entirely destroy the beaver's strong dam.

Shaggycoat's grandfather, being very old, and wise according to his years, took the lead, and the younger beaver followed, keeping close to the tail of his guide. They swam near the bottom and were careful to avoid the bright light of the great fires that men had built upon the ice in many places to prevent their escape.

By the time the moon had risen they were near the upper end of the lake. They at once took refuge in an old burrow that the trappers had overlooked and lay still until the moon went under a cloud when they came out and crept along the bank, still going under the ice. When the moon appeared again they hid under the roots of a tree that made a sort of natural burrow. There they lay for all the world like the ends of two black logs, until a friendly cloud again obscured the moon when they pushed on. Once the trappers came very near to them when they were hiding behind some stones, waiting for a friendly cloud, and Shaggycoat was about to dash away and betray their whereabouts, when his grandfather nipped him severely in the shoulder which kept him still, and alone saved his fine glossy coat.

They were now getting well up into the river that had supplied their lake, and it was not so easy to find breathing places as it had been in the lake where the water was low. But they could usually find some crack or crevice or some point where there were a few inches between the water and the ice and where they could fill their lungs before they journeyed on.

They had come so far and so fast that poor Shaggycoat's legs ached with the ceaseless motion, but the older beaver gave him no rest, and led him on and on, swimming with easy, steady strokes. Although his own legs were weary and a bit rheumatic, he valued his life more than he did his legs and so set his teeth and breasted the current bravely. They both held their fore paws close up under them and used their hind legs entirely for propelling themselves, so these had to do double duty, plying away like the screw wheel on a great steamer.

When Shaggycoat remonstrated against going any farther, saying in beaver language that his legs were ready to drop off, his senior reminded him that his skin would drop off if they stopped, and, with a new wild terror tugging at his heart, he fled on.

When daylight came, they had covered five good English miles up the river, and were nearly eight miles from their dam and the beautiful woodland lake that had been their home.

Then the old beaver began looking for some burrow or overhanging bank where they might hide during the day and get some sleep, of which they were in great need. Finally they found a suitable place where the bank had shelved in, leaving a natural den, high and dry above the water. Here they rested and passed the day, getting nothing better to eat than a few frozen lily stems and some dead bark from a log that had been frozen into the ice. The dry lifeless bark was not much like the tender juicy bark that they were used to, but it helped a little to still the gnawings of hunger, and in this retreat they soon fell asleep and slept nearly the whole of the day.

But the older beaver was always watchful, sleeping with one eye open, as you might say, and waking very easily.

Once, when he was awakened by a sense of danger, he saw a large otter swim leisurely by their hiding-place and his heart beat hard and fast until he was out of sight, for he knew that if the otter discovered them, he would at once attack them and the battle would probably end in his favor.

Shaggycoat would be of little help in a real fight for life and the old beaver was far past his prime, his teeth being dull and broken. When the otter was out of sight, the watchman lay down and resumed his nap.

When Shaggycoat awoke, he knew it was evening for he could

plainly see the stars shining through the ice.

His legs were cramped and stiff and there was a gnawing sensation in the region of his stomach, but there was nothing in sight to eat. His grandfather informed him in beaver language that there were weary miles to cover before they could rest again.

As soon as it was fairly dark, they came out from under the overhanging bank that had shielded them so nicely during the day and resumed their journey, swimming like two ocean liners, on and on. Their track was not as straight as that of the boats would have been, for they dodged in and out, going where the darker ice and projecting banks gave them cover, and stopping when they scented danger.

When they had gone about a mile, they found a spot where the river had set back over the bank, freezing in some alder bushes. Upon the stems of these they made a scant meal and went on feeling a bit better. This night seemed longer and wearier to Shaggycoat than the first had. He was not so fresh and the first excitement was over, but the old beaver would not let him rest as he knew their only safety lay in putting a long distance between them and their destroyers.

They were not so fortunate in finding a hiding-place as they had been the day before, but they finally took refuge in a deserted otter's burrow, which made them a very good nest, although it was possible that some wandering otter might happen in, and dispossess them.

When night again came round, they made a light supper on frozen lily stems and pushed on. They covered less distance that night than they had done before, for both were feeling the strain of the long flight, and so they rested frequently and took more time to hunt for food.

About daybreak of this third night of their journey, they found an open place in the ice where the stream was rapid and went ashore; here they soon satisfied their hunger upon the bark of the poplar and birch.

When they had made a good meal, the prudent old beaver, assisted by Shaggycoat, felled several small poplars and cutting them in pieces about three feet long dragged them under the ice to a protected bank and hid them against the time of need, for he had decided to spend a few days where they were, getting the rest and sleep which they both needed.

CHAPTER II

ALONE IN THE WORLD

For two or three weeks the beavers kept very quiet in their new retreat, only going out at night, which is their usual habit. They replenished their food of birch and poplar bark frequently by felling small saplings, cutting them up in pieces about three feet in length and then securing them under the ice.

This was great fun for Shaggycoat, who had never done any work before and he loved to see the tall saplings come swishing down, but it was no fun for his grandfather who was getting very old. The long flight, the loss of sleep, and want of food, had been too much for him, and he did not recuperate as quickly as the two-year-old.

One day just at dusk, Shaggycoat thought he would steal out and fell a tree for himself. His teeth fairly ached to be gnawing something, so he slipped away from his grandfather and paddled out to the open spot in the ice. Although he is a great swimmer and is only excelled by the otter, the beaver does not swim like other quadrupeds, for he holds his forefeet up under him, and works his powerful hind legs like lightning. As the feet are broad and webbed and he strikes at a slight angle, he propels himself through the water with great velocity.

As Shaggycoat neared the open place in the river where the water ran swiftly and it was easy to clamber out on the bank, a queer feeling came over him.

He was not afraid to go out alone, although his grandfather had always gone with him. It was only a few steps and he thought nothing could harm him, but something seemed to hold him back and fill him with a sense of danger. Then he happened to glance up and, close to the opening in the ice, he saw a large gray animal crouched, watching the hole intently.

The stranger was two or three times the size of Shaggycoat, as large as any beaver he had ever seen, but he was not a beaver. His fore paws were too long and powerful, his head with tufted ears too flat, and his eyes were too cruel and hungry. The longer Shaggycoat looked at the fierce animal above him on the ice, the greater grew his fear, until he fled at a headlong pace to the overhanging bank, where his grandfather was sleeping. His precipitate flight into the burrow awoke the old beaver who slept lightly and was always watchful.

When Shaggycoat related his adventure, the old beaver looked troubled and combed his head thoughtfully with the claws upon his hind leg. After dusk had fallen and the stars appeared, he carefully reconnoitred, leaving Shaggycoat in the burrow. After half an hour's time, he returned and his manner was anxious.

He told Shaggycoat that they must not use the opening in the ice any more or go upon the land, for a lynx had found their hiding-place and would watch by their front door until he dined upon beaver meat. They must start that very night and go farther up the river and find a new opening, and even then they must be cautious. This was sorrowful news for them both and the younger beaver remonstrated against leaving their fine store of bark, but he got a sharp nip in his ear and was told to keep his advice until it was asked for. So, after making a hearty supper, they went sorrowfully upon their way to find a new open spot in the river where the lynx would not be watching for them.

They went only about a mile that night, but found several open spots for the ice was getting ready to break up. At last, they found a place that suited them and dragged themselves up under a sheltering bank, near a rapid, that afforded them a chance to go in search of food. Then the old beaver slept long and sound, leaving Shaggycoat upon guard with orders to wake him if anything uncommon appeared.

The young beaver did not like these silent vigils and the hours seemed very long to him, but he did as he was told. He thought his grandfather never would wake, but at last he did, late in the afternoon, but they did not go ashore for bark--it was too dangerous, the older beaver said--so they had a slim supper of frozen lily pads. But this was not enough for the hungry stomach of Shaggycoat who gnawed away at some tree roots that pierced the bank where they were hiding. It was not as good as the fresh bark of the birch, but it filled him up and made him feel better.

If Shaggycoat had been older and wiser, he would have been alarmed at the old beaver's symptoms, but he was young and thoughtless, and knew not of age, or the signs of failing life.

At last the spring freshet came and the ice in the river broke up. Then they had to look for a spot where the bank was very high so they would not be drowned out. It was a long and arduous search to find the right spot, but at last it was found just in time, for the old beaver's strength was nearly spent. But every day that the snow melted and the ice went out of the river, food for the beavers grew more plentiful and the sunshine and hope of spring made them glad.

Shaggycoat was now left to himself, to swim in the river and feed upon the bark of saplings along the shore. The old beaver was too tired with their long journey to venture out of the burrow they had chosen. He gave Shaggycoat much good advice, and among other things told him to always keep close to the water where he was comparatively safe, while upon land, he was the easy prey of all his natural enemies. The peculiar angle of his hind legs made it impossible for him, or any other beaver, to travel much on shore, but, while in the water they were his safeguard.

These were delightful days for the two-year-old. The water was getting warm and the mere act of swimming filled him with delight. Besides, it seemed like a very wonderful world in which he lived. He had come so far and seen so many strange things. He wondered if there were other rivers and if they were all as long as this one.

One spring morning when the air was warm and balmy and birds had begun to sing in the tree-tops along the bank, Shaggycoat went for a swim in a deep pool. It was not his custom to be abroad in the daylight, for beavers as a rule love the dark and do most of their work in inky darkness, but the two-year-old felt restless. He must be stirring. His grandfather was too old and stupid for him, so he went.

He had a delightful play and a good breakfast upon some alders that grew in a little cove. He stayed much longer than usual, so that when he returned the sun was low in the west.

He found his grandfather stretched out much as he had left him, but there was something peculiar about him. He was so still. He was not sleeping, for there was no motion of the chest and no steam from the nostrils. Shaggycoat went up to him and put his nose to his, but it was quite cold. Then he poked him gently with his paw, but he did not stir. Then he nipped his ear as the older beaver had so frequently done to him, but there was no response.

He would wait; perhaps this was a new kind of sleep. He would probably wake in the morning, but a strange uneasiness filled Shaggycoat. He was almost afraid of his grandfather, for he was so quiet and his nose was so cold.

He waited an hour or two and then tried to waken him again, but with no better success. This time to touch the icy nose of the old beaver sent a chill through Shaggycoat's every nerve, and a sudden terror of the lifeless silent thing before him seized him.

Then a sense of loss, coupled with a great fear, came over him and he fled from the burrow like a hunted creature. He must put as many miles as possible between himself and that sleep from which there was no waking.

The river had never seemed so dark and uninviting before, nor held so many terrors. His grandfather had always led the way and he had merely to follow. Now he was to lead. But where? He did not know the way, but that silence and the terror of that stiff form with the cold nose haunted him and he fled on.

Morning found him many miles from the shelving bank, where the old beaver had been left behind.

Shaggycoat feared the river and all it contained. The world too was strange to him, but most of all he feared that silent form under the dark bank.

From that day he became a wanderer in the great world. He went by river courses and through mountain lakes, always keeping out of danger as well as he could.

Many scraps of good advice he now remembered which had been given him by his grandfather. Perhaps his grandfather had felt the heavy sleep coming upon him and had given the advice that Shaggycoat might take care of himself when he should be left alone; or maybe it was only an instinct that had come down through many generations of aquatic builders. But certain things he did and others he refrained from doing, because something told him that it would be dangerous.

Other bits of information he gathered from sad experience. Many things befell him that probably never would, had he been in company with wiser heads, but, he was an orphan, and the lot of the orphan is always hard.

These are a few of the lessons that he learned during that adventurous summer: that the water is the beaver's element, but on land he is the laughing-stock of all who behold him; that in the water is comparative safety, but on land are many dangers; that the otter is the beaver's deadly enemy, always to be avoided if possible; that minks and muskrats are harmless little creatures, but not suitable company for a self-respecting beaver; that sweet-smelling meat, for which you do not have to work, is dangerous and bites like a clam, holding on even more persistently.

These and other things too numerous to mention Shaggycoat learned, some by observation and some by personal experience.

At first, the summer passed quickly. There were so many things to see, and so many rivers and lakes to visit, but by degrees a sense of loneliness came over him. He had no friend, no companion.

He was positively alone in all the great world.

CHAPTER III

THE COURTSHIP OF SHAGGYCOAT

My young readers may wonder why I have called the beaver, whose fortunes we are following, Shaggycoat, so I will tell them.

The fur of the beaver and the otter is very thick and soft, but, in its natural state, it is quite different from what it is when worn by women in cloaks and coats, for the fine short fur is sprinkled with long hairs that give the coat a shaggy, uneven appearance. In the case of our own beaver, Shaggycoat, these long hairs were very pronounced, so you see the name fitted him nicely.

When the fur of any of these little animals is prepared for market, the long hairs are all pulled out with a small pair of tweezers. This is called plucking the skin.

As the summer days went by and August ripened into September, the loneliness that had oppressed Shaggycoat during the summer grew tenfold and he became more restless than ever. There seemed to be something for which he was looking and longing. It was not right that he should wander up and down lakes and streams and have no living creatures to stop to speak with him. His world was too large; the lakes and streams were too endless. He wanted to share them with somebody or something. He had found many a wondrous water nook, which he would like to show some one; but still up and down he wandered, and no one did he find to share his great world. Yet it seemed sometimes as though he had come near to somebody or something, for which he was looking, but it always vanished at the next turn of the stream or at the waterfall.

Thus in this endless searching that came to naught, like searching for the pot of gold at the end of the rainbow, the autumn days passed.

The maples and the oaks shook out their crimson and golden streamers, and a touch of surpassing glory was on all the world. Sometimes the merry wind would shower down maple leaves until the edge of the stream was as bright as the boughs above.

It seemed that their fire touched Shaggycoat as he swam among them, making him burn and glow like the autumn forest.

Then a new plan came into his wise head. If what he was looking for could not be found by searching, perhaps it might be coaxed to come to him. He would try and see. So he gathered some grass and mud and made a very queer patty, which looked much like a child's mud pie. This he smoothed off with as much care as a baker would a cream cake.

This patty had been made by a beaver. He was sure that whoever found it would know that, for it had a strong musky smell, so he left his love-letter under a bush near a watercourse, and went away to wait developments.

A day he waited, but his letter remained unopened, and, of course, unread. Two days, and no better result, but the third day he found to his great joy that the letter had been opened. There was an unmistakable beaver musk about it, and new paw and nose prints upon it.

This was his answer. It said as plainly as words could have said, "I have read your letter and know what it means. I am waiting in some pool, or under a shelving bank near-by. Come."

Then Shaggycoat raced up and down the stream churning the water like a tug boat, until he found fresh beaver tracks in the mud. These he followed rapidly along the bank until he came to where it overhung the water and there he found his mate waiting for him with glad eyes.

Shaggycoat went up to her and rubbed his nose against hers. It was not like his grandfather's nose, cold and repellent, but warm and caressing. He backed away a pace or two to look at her and there was new joy in his heart.

She was not quite as large as he, and her coat was just a shade lighter drab, but she was very sleek and Shaggycoat was well satisfied.

I know not what they said there under the shelving bank, during their first tryst, but I do not agree with those niggardly naturalists who would strip the brute kingdom of feeling and intelligence and the power to express joy and pain, and appropriate all these feelings to themselves.

It may be that Shaggycoat told his newly found mate how bright her eyes were and how long he had searched for her or perhaps she confessed that she had seen him many times just around the bend in the stream, but had not thought that he was looking for her. We are none of us certain of any of these things, but we are sure of one thing. It was a very happy meeting.

Then Shaggycoat led the way through lake and river to many wonderful water grottoes; to deep pools where the bottom of the lake was as dark and forbidding as midnight, or to shallows, where the bottom of the stream was gay with bright pebbles, and where the sunlight danced upon the uneven water until it made a wondrous many colored mirror.

He showed her his waterfall, and a part of a small dam that he had constructed just for fun across a little brook. The waterfall was not really his any more than it was any one else's, but he called it his.

These and many other water wonders he showed his young mate, and her eyes grew brighter as the wonders of their world grew. She wondered how he had traveled so far, and seen so many things. But all the time Shaggycoat was leading the way toward a dear little brook that he knew of away back in the wilderness, in one of the fastnesses of nature. He had a definite plan in his head concerning this stream. He had made it weeks before and arranged many of its details. But one day as they journeyed, a sad accident befell Brighteyes, and for a time it bade fair to end all their hopes.

They were swimming leisurely up stream and had stopped at the mouth of a little rill where the water was very fresh, when Brighteyes discovered a stick of sweet smelling birch hanging just above the water's edge. It fairly made her mouth water.

But Shaggycoat was suspicious. He had seen wood fixed like this before. He had tasted it and something had caught him by the paw, and only after several hours of wrenching had he been able to free himself. Even then he had left one claw and a part of the toe in the trap.

So he pushed Brighteyes from the trap and tried to hurry away with her. But, with true feminine wilfulness and curiosity, she persisted, and a moment later the trap was sprung and she was held fast by the toes of one of her forefeet.

She tugged and twisted, pulled and turned in every direction, but it would not let go. Then Shaggycoat got hold of the chain with his teeth and pulled too, but with no better success.

Brighteyes struggled until her paw was nearly wrenched from the shoulder, but the persistent thing that held her by three toes still clung like a vise.

At last when both beavers were filled with despair, and a wild terror of being held so firmly had seized them, a bright idea came to Shaggycoat. He gnawed off the stake that held the chain upon the trap and his mate was free to go, with the trap still clinging to her paw, and the chain rattling along upon the stones. Then they tried all sorts of experiments to get the trap off, the two most ingenious ways being drowning it, and burying it in the mud, and then seeking to steal away quietly without disturbing it. But the trap was not to be taken unawares in this way, and always followed. Finally it caught between two stones where the brook was shallow, and came off itself. You may imagine they were glad to see the last of it, and Brighteyes never forgot the lesson.

It was several days before her shoulder got fairly over the wrenching, but it may have saved her glossy coat in after years.

Finally, after traveling leisurely for about a week, they came to the mountain stream that Shaggycoat had in mind. It wound through a broad alder covered meadow, with steep foothills a mile or so back on either side. The meadow was about two miles long and at the lower end, where the stream ran into a narrow valley, there were two large pines, one on either bank.

Up in the foothills were innumerable birch and maple saplings and here and there in the meadow were knolls of higher land, covered with small pines and spruces.

Perhaps Shaggycoat had seen this wild meadow covered with water in the spring during a freshet, or maybe he had only imagined it, but there was a picture in his active mind of a strong beaver dam at the foot of the narrows and a broad lake that should be enclosed by the foothills; upon the islands were to be many beaver lodges, the first of which should be occupied by Brighteyes and himself.

CHAPTER IV

HOW THE GREAT DAM WAS BUILT

Shaggycoat, of course, had had no experience in dam-building, but he had often watched repairs upon the dam in the colony where he and his grandfather lived, before that terrible winter and the destruction of their snug city. He was too young at the time to be allowed to help in such important work as strengthening the dam, which needed old and wise heads, but there was no rule against his watching and seeing how it was done.

He had planned to model his dam in the alder meadow after the one at the old colony.

He had traveled many weary miles by lakes and rivers, to find a spot where such a dam could be built. A broad meadow surrounded by foothills, with a narrow neck at the lower end where the dam was to be, and large trees near to use in its construction. There were many places where the ordinary dams, made of short sections of logs, piled up like a cob house, could be built. The brush and stone dam could also be made almost anywhere, but the kind Shaggycoat wanted, which was easier to make than any other could be built only in certain places, so he had chosen the spot with great care.

His observation of repairs on the old dam would stand him in good stead, but even had he not seen this work, it is probable that his beaver's building instinct would have supplied the needed knowledge. His kind had been dam builders for ages.

It was the beaver dams of the eighteenth century that gave us most of our pleasant meadows, where hay and crops now grow so plentifully. Originally these lowlands were covered with timber, but the beaver dams overflowed the valleys, and made them fertile. This also killed off the timber, which finally rotted and fell into the water, and the meadow was cleared as effectually as though the settlers had done it with their axes. Traces of these dams may still be found.

Just to illustrate how ingrained the building instinct is in the beaver: a young beaver was held in captivity in the third story of an apartment house in London. There were no sticks, no mud, nor anything to suggest building. He had no parents to teach him this industry, yet he soon set to work and built brushes, shoes, hassocks, and anything else movable that he could get hold of into a wall across one corner of the room. This was his dam.

One October evening, when the harvest moon was at its full and its mellow radiance shimmered on tree-top and water, and the world was like a beautiful dream, half in light, half in shadow, Shaggycoat and Brighteyes took their places at the foot of one of the great pines at the lower end of the meadow and the work of dam-building began. But just how they set to work you could never guess, unless you are familiar with the habits of these most interesting animals.

They stood upon their hind legs, balancing themselves nicely upon their broad flat tails, and began nipping a ring about the tree. It was not a very deep cut, and looked for all the world like the girdle that the nurseryman makes upon his apple trees, only it was a little more ragged. When the tree had been circled, they began again about three inches above the first girdle, and cut another. When they touched noses again at the farther side of the tree, they began pulling out the chips between the two girdles. When this operation had been completed for the entire circumference of the tree, they had made the first cut which was about three inches broad, and perhaps a half an inch deep, for they had the bark to help them, and this was the easiest cut on the tree.

Do you imagine that they stopped for a frolic when the first cut had been made, as many boys or girls would have done? Not a bit of it, for they knew better than man could have told them how soon cold weather would make work upon the dam impossible, and there was the lodge to build after the dam had been made.

You would have laughed if you had seen these two comparatively small animals at the foot of that giant pine, nipping away at it like persistent little wood-choppers. The old tree was tall and majestic. It had withstood the winds of a century, and its heart was still stout. The chips that they took were so small, and the task before them so great, but, if you had happened by the following day and seen the furrow, some two or three inches in depth, you would have marveled, and not been so sure of the old pine's ability to withstand these ambitious rodents.

Night after night they worked, and once or twice they had to widen the cut, which had become so narrow that they could not get their heads in to work, but, even as water wears away stone by constant action, they wore away the stout heart of the old pine.

At last, one morning, just as the moon was setting and the pale stars were fading, a shudder ran through the tall pine and it quivered as they cut through the last fibres of its strong heart. A moment it tottered like an old man upon his staff, then swayed, as though uncertain which way to go, and fell with a rush of wind and a roar that resounded from foothill to foothill until the meadow echoed with the downfall of the old sentinel.

It had fallen squarely across the stream, just as they had hoped. This was probably not through any prowess of the beavers as woodsmen, but nearly all timber that grows upon the bank of a stream leans toward the water, owing to the fact that trees grow more freely upon that side.

The sun was now rising, so they left their work, well pleased that the tree was down, but by dusk they were at it again.

The trunk of the pine, and particularly its thick foliage, had dammed the water somewhat, so it was already beginning to set back, but most of it trickled through and went upon its way rejoicing at its escape. Some large limbs upon the tree still held it several feet from the ground, so they set to work on the under side of the tree, cutting off the limbs and lowering the trunk to just the height they wished. Some of this work had to be done under water, but that is no hardship for a beaver, for he can stay under several minutes. When breathing had become difficult they would come up, bringing the severed limbs in their teeth. These would be jammed into the mud just in front of the tree trunk, like the pickets upon a fence. If you had tried to pull out one of these limbs after they had once planted it, you would have found it a difficult task.

In two nights they lowered the pine to the desired height, and made it look like a dam.

The following night, they began upon the other pine on the opposite bank, and girdled it as they had done the first. The tree looked lonely now with its mate gone. Perhaps it felt so and did not care that the sharp teeth were nipping away at its bark, or maybe it still longed to battle with the elements, and this spasmodic pain in its sap filled it with forebodings.

As relentlessly as they had gnawed away at the first tree, they worked at the second until it, too, fell with a rush of air, the snap of breaking branches and a thunderous thud that shook the valley. They were not as fortunate this time as they had been before and though the pine fell across the stream, it fell further up than its mate, leaving a gap between them.

You could never guess how they remedied this mishap. They certainly could not move the tree, but that was really what they did, for they gnawed off the limbs that supported it on the down-stream side, and it rolled over of its own weight, so that in this way the gap was filled. The structure now looked quite like the outline of a dam.

Then work upon it was suspended for a time and they went up-stream about twenty rods and dug three holes in a knoll that would soon be an island, for the reason that the water was now setting back quite rapidly. These holes were started near the bank of the stream running back under ground for several feet, and then turning upward and coming out at the surface. Three such holes were dug, each leading to a different place near the bank of the stream, but all coming out at the same spot at the top of the knoll.

They soon resumed work upon the dam and small trees and brush might have been seen floating down the stream, guided by industrious beavers, who gave the material a shove here and a push there to keep it in the current. Now that the dam was beginning to flow the meadows, they would make the stream do their carrying just as it did cargoes for man.

The brush and saplings were stuck vertically in front of the pine barricade, and the holes between were plastered up with mud and sods, until the structure was fairly tight. The mud they carried in their fore paws hugged up under the chin, or on the broad tail which made a fine trowel with which to smooth it off.

Little by little the holes on the dam were filled, until finally it was quite smooth and symmetrical. It could be built larger and stronger the next year, but for this year they only needed a small pond that should make a primitive Venice for them, and shield their lodge from a land attack. By the time the first hard freeze came, the dam had been completed for that year, and the freeze strengthened it just as they had intended.

A beautiful little lake about a quarter of a mile in length, and half as wide, now shimmered and sparkled in the valley and the beavers were glad that they had been so prospered.

CHAPTER V

A BEAVER LODGE

It will be remembered that before beginning work on the dam the beavers went to a point a few rods above where it was to be placed and dug three holes running back from the stream. These holes started at different points in the bank but all converged at the top of the knoll.

The water had now set back and covered the lower end of the holes near the stream, but the opening at the top of the knoll was high and dry.

The beavers now set to work with mud, sticks, stones, fine brush, and weeds, and built a circular wall about eight feet in diameter around the hole at the top of the knoll. The wall was about two feet thick and during the first two or three days of building looked for all the world like the snow fort that children build by rolling huge snowballs into a circular wall, and then plastering in the cracks with loose snow, only the beavers' work was more regular and symmetrical than that of the children.

It was now the first of November and freezing a little each night; just the best time imaginable for a beaver to work upon his house, for it was really a house that the beavers were building.

While the November sky was bright with stars, and the milky way was luminous; while the frost scaled over the edges of their little pond, and the fresh north winds rapidly stripped the forest of its last leaves, the beavers worked upon their house with that industry which is proverbial of them.

They brought mud in their paws or on their broad flat tails, and sticks and brush in their teeth and plastered away like skilful masons. When a pile of mud had been placed in the proper position, it would be smoothed off carefully with the patient fore paws or perhaps that broad strong tail would come down upon it with a resounding slap and the trick was done.

When the wall began to round over for the roof, the difficulty began. Here they had to put in rafters. These were formed of pliable sticks of alder or willow, one end being stuck in the mud wall, and the other bent over at the top, until all came together where the chimney would be just like the poles in an Indian's wigwam. Here they also had to use great care in placing the mud, for it would frequently fall through between the rafters, or slide down upon them. If they could work, when it was freezing, the cold froze the mud to the rafters and helped to keep it in place. Several times, part of the roof fell in and had to be relaid, but they still worked away and, finally, all but a very small opening, two or three inches in diameter, had been closed. This opening was the vent or chimney, where foul air might escape. This hole had to be just large enough to permit the escape of hot air, but not large enough to admit any of their enemies.

The same night that the final touches were put upon the roof of this curious dome-shaped house, the ground froze hard, and in the morning the wall of Mr. and Mrs. Beaver's new abode was quite substantial. But later on when the hard freeze had made the earth like rock, this little mud house would be a veritable fortress, capable of withstanding almost any onset with ordinary weapons. Even a man with a crowbar and axe would have found it a hard task to enter this stronghold of these queer little people.

So you see the beaver had planned his work well and the frost and the wind had helped him. He had harnessed the stream to do his work, and made its water protect him from his enemies. Just as men built their castles in days of old, the beaver had made his dam, so that a moat should surround his house, where the drawbridge should always be up, and the only way of entrance or exit should be by water.

You may wonder how after the roof of their house had been closed up, and no door left, the beavers went to and from their dwelling, but do you not remember the three holes that had been dug several weeks before. These were now their three submerged channels to the outer world, through which only a good swimmer could pass. This was the way they went. A plunge down the hole at the centre of the lodge, and a dark form would shoot out at the bank of the river. Perhaps a beaver's head, dripping with water would be poked up, only a few feet from the mud house, or maybe they would go the entire width of the pond before coming to the surface, for they are great swimmers, and can stay down for several minutes without coming to the surface to breathe.

Besides having three doors through which to escape to their water world, the beavers took other precautions against being entrapped in their snug house, or caught in the pond without a place of refuge to flee to.

They searched the bank for places where it was steep or shelving, overhanging the water. At such points they dug burrows back into the bank, gradually running them upward, but stopping a foot or two short of the surface. Here they would scoop out a snug burrow or nest to which they could retreat when living in the house became dangerous. They made three or four such burrows, the lower end of each being under water, and the nest end high and dry, but still underground. By this time they felt that their pond was fairly well fortified, and they set to work, laying in their winter store of food, for they knew that the pond would soon freeze over thus making them prisoners under the ice for the entire winter, so they must make their plans accordingly.

They went to the upper end of the pond and began felling birch, poplar and maple saplings, three or four inches in diameter. These small trees they limbed out, and cut up into pieces about three feet in length, just as a wood-chopper would cut cord wood.

When a tree had been cut up into these convenient pieces, one of the beavers would load it upon the shoulders of the other, who would cling to the stick with his teeth, and they would begin dragging it to the water. The beaver usually went obliquely, dragging the stick after him, with one end trailing. When it had been rolled into the water, it was left to the current which they knew would float it down to the dam. If the channel became blocked and logs lodged along the shore, they pushed them off like the good log-men they were.

It took two or three weeks to cut the winter's supply of wood, which was not for fuel but food. All the logs had been floated down to the dam and secured under water near the lodge, when the great freeze came. It was quite difficult to make the sticks stay under water, but this they managed to do in several ways. Some of them they thrust into the mud, while others were secured under roots, and a large pile was made safe at the dam by thrusting one stick under another and allowing the top sticks to keep the under ones down.

One clear, crisp night, about the first of December, the North Wind awoke and came galloping over the frozen fields, bringing with him legions of frost folks. The fingers of these myriad little people were like icicles, and everything that they touched was congealed. They found the beavers' pond, and danced a merry dance over the sparkling water, and every time that they stooped to touch the clear water, crystals of ice formed and spread in every direction.

It had been a very pleasant autumn, but the North Wind was angry to-night, and he howled like a demon, and smote lake and river with his icy mittens, so that when the sun rose next morning, lakes and streams were cased in a glittering armor of ice and the beavers were prisoners for the winter.

For the next four or five months they would live under ice, but they did not care about that. It was what they had planned and worked for for weeks. They were snugly housed with plenty of tender bark for their winter's food, so the wind might howl, and the frost freeze. It would only strengthen their barricade and make them more secure against the outer world.

In their thick-walled house it was quite snug. The heat of their bodies made it warm and the vent at the top carried off the foul air. Whenever they were tired of confinement, they would go for a swim in the pond through one of the three sub-marine passages, just as though the pond had not been frozen over. The only care that they needed to exercise was to look out that these holes did not ice over and thus lock them in their lodge like rats in a trap. To prevent this, they broke the ice frequently with their tails during cold days. Some cold nights they were obliged to watch the holes for hours to prevent them from freezing.

It was twilight of a bleak December day. The sun had taken his accustomed plunge behind the western horizon, but still shone blood red upon the clouds above the gray hills. There was still light enough from the afterglow to cast shadows, and phantom shapes peopled the aisles of the forest, or stretched their long arms across the fields.

The moon was just rising in the east, and it made shadows and shapes uncanny and unearthly. Already the heavens were studded with stars, and the wind moaned fitfully, rattling down snow and ice and whistling in the leafless twigs.

Down from the foothills, coming like a wary hunter, a wildcat prowled to the edge of the beavers' pond. A part of the way he had followed a rabbit's track, but it had proved so old that he had finally given it up. When he hurried he moved by quick jumps, bringing down all four feet at a time quite close together, and leaving those four telltale paw-prints in a bunch that hunters know so well. When he wanted to be more cautious, he walked cat-like, setting his fore paw down as softly as though his foot were velvet. He was an ugly looking brute, rather heavily built, with a thick head, and square topped club ears that usually lay back close to his head. His visage was generously sprinkled with whiskers, but it was accented by two hungry yellow green eyes, that seemed almost phosphorescent. His habitual expression was a snarl.

At the edge of the beaver pond, he tried the wind this way and that. His nostrils dilated, his eyes snapped fire, and his stump of a tail twitched. There was game abroad. He knew that scent of old. It was quite common away to the north from whence he had wandered. Cautiously he crept forward, putting down his paws in the dainty cat-like manner; but he must have known that the beavers were out of his reach at this time of year. Perhaps his hunger made him forgetful or he may have looked for the unexpected.

Half-way across the pond he stopped and sniffed again; it was close at hand now. Then he noticed the conical house on the island near, and crept cautiously toward it. Twice he walked about the house, which was now partly covered with snow, then with one jump he landed upon the very dome of the beavers' dwelling and peeked in at the air hole. What he saw made saliva drip from his mouth and his eyes dilate. There within three feet of his death-dealing paws were a pair of sleek beavers, warm and cozy. The hot scent fairly ravished his nostrils. It was unendurable, and he tore at the frozen mud house like a fury, first with his fore paws, then with his powerful hind paws armed with one of the best set of claws in the New England woods. But it was as hard as a stone wall and the beavers might just as well have been miles away as far as he was concerned.

Then the wildcat peeked in again, and ungovernable rage seized him. He reared upon his haunches, and beat the air with his fore paws and howled and shrieked like a demon. The beavers started from their twilight nap with sudden terror. This fury that was tearing at their house and filling the night with awful sounds seemed almost upon their very backs, so they fled precipitately through the water passages into the pond and took refuge in one of the burrows along the bank.

A moment later when the wildcat again peeped in at the vent, the house was quite empty. Then after a few more futile efforts to break through the frozen walls he went away, going from bush to bush, alert and watchful. Only the tracks remained to tell that the beavers had had so unwelcome a caller.

CHAPTER VI

HOW THE WINTER WENT

December came and went, and the first of the new year found the beavers snugly caught beneath a barricade of six inches of ice. The water from the little brook that fed their pond was very clear, so that the ice was as transparent as glass. This enabled them to see what was going on outside almost as well as they could before the ice had formed, and besides, it kept out the wind and the cold.

You may wonder at this, and think that no place on earth could be colder than the bottom of an ice-bound pond; but I am sure that a thermometer under water would have registered much higher temperature than one above, for if this were not so, the water would freeze solid to the bottom.

Did you ever have your playmates bury you in the snow just for fun? The snow looks cold, and seems uninviting, but once snugly tucked away in it, it is quite a warm white blanket. People of northern latitudes frequently save their lives, when caught out in a cold storm, by covering themselves in the snow. In the same manner the dog teams in Alaska pass the bitter cold nights of an arctic winter buried in the snow. So the ice made the beavers' pond snug in the same manner.

Besides being warmed by its coating of ice, the frost folks had also made the pond very beautiful. Wherever there was an uneven spot in the ice, the sunlight was broken into a wonderful rainbow prism of dazzling colors, that showed more plainly under the ice than above. There were green, blue, opal, and many shades of light red, all of which made a beautiful roof for the beavers' winter palace.

In addition to this, all the grasses and reeds along the edge of the pond were gemmed with ice-diamonds. These globules of ice caught the sun's rays, and in many cases refracted them as brilliantly as real diamonds would have done. In all the little inlets where reeds and flags had been frozen into the ice, the frost folks had played queer pranks, so that the pond was a most beautiful place, as well as a very snug one.

The phrase "as busy as a beaver" was anything but descriptive of their life now, for they did little but sleep and eat bark. They had provided well for these cold months, and now they had nothing to do but enjoy themselves. I am inclined to think that the maxim about working like a beaver only applies to two or three months in the autumn, for the rest of the year the beaver is a very lazy fellow. All through the winter months he sleeps in his snug house, or nibbles away at his store of bark. Then, as soon as the ice breaks up, all the male beavers over three years of age start on their annual wanderings through lakes and streams. There is no particular object in this quest, but it is just a nomadic habit, an impulse that stirs in the blood, as soon as the sap starts in the maple, and keeps them moving until some time in September.

One day must have been very much like another under their covering of ice. Inside the lodge, the diameter was three or four feet and about the same in height. Each beaver has his own particular bed, which he always occupies, and the house is kept very neat and clean. I do not imagine there was much regularity in their meals, but whenever they felt hungry, one would go to the pile of logs near the dam and select a piece. This was then dragged into the lodge and peeled leisurely. When it was white and shining, it was taken back and thrust into some crevice in the dam, or piled by itself. It had served its turn, and was now discarded.

One enemy the beavers had who gave them considerable annoyance and some anxiety. This was the gluttonous wolverine, which is a mongrel wolf, meaner than any other member of the family. His prey is small animals, and his particular delicacy is beaver meat. He is also a lover of carrion and dark deeds, and is altogether a despicable fellow.

The crowning event in the life of the beaver lodge during that first winter, was the coming of four fuzzy, awkward, beaver babies. They were very queer looking little chaps, with long, clumsy hind legs, which they never knew quite how to use until they were shown the mysteries of the water world and swimming. These mites of beavers were not as well clad as their parents, for their fur was very short, but they nestled close to their mother, and, by dint of wriggling into her warm coat, kept warm until spring.

Shaggycoat was much busier after the young beavers came. He now had to bring all the wood into the lodge, for Brighteyes stuck close to her children and Shaggycoat was glad to wait upon her. So, when she was hungry, he brought logs into the mud house and peeled them for her.

Several times during the winter, they heard sounds of some animal digging at the outer wall of their castle, and occasionally an ugly looking wolfish muzzle was thrust in at the vent, which at first gave them great uneasiness, but, by degrees, this wore away, as they found out how strong the house was and how little the digging of their enemy accomplished.

At last the spring rains came, and the ice began to break up. Then, as the water rose, and the ice was tumbled about by the current, which was swollen, there were loud reports from the cracking ice that echoed across the valley, just as they had when the great pines fell.

Huge cakes of ice were piled upon their island, and one struck the mud house, threatening to demolish it, but it withstood the shock.

The dam was severely tried during these spring freshets. The ice pounded and ground away at it, and the water set back, until the pond was twice the size it had been in the autumn. The beavers were nearly drowned out of their lodge during this high water, but finally a portion of the dam gave way and the water fell. Then the ice went churning and scraping through the break. Driftwood and brush and all sorts of debris came down with the flood, and the water was full of silt and gravel. The pond was not the crystal lake it had been.

It gradually settled, and things looked as they had in the autumn; the trees were leafless, and the landscape cheerless. The pond also froze over along the edges at night and thawed by day.

Away down in the heart of the earth, the secret forces of nature were stirring. The maple had already felt the touch of life, and its sap coursed gleefully in its veins. The awakening had not come yet, but it was coming. The flowers and the buds had been sleeping, the nuts and the seeds had been waiting patiently, but their time of waiting was nearly over.

Already daffodil and arbutus stirred uneasily in their slumber. Their dreams were light, like the sleep of early morning. Into their dreams would steal a sense of soft winds and warm sunshine.

Then, one day, the sense of this life about them became so certain, and their dreams were so real, that they awoke, and spring had really come. Up they sprang like children who had overslept and opened their hearts to the joy of living in the warmth of the new spring.

Now the pond was no longer frozen over along the bank, but the shores were very muddy with the coming out of the frost. Soon birds began to sing in the bushes along the pond, and a sense of restlessness came over Shaggycoat, for everything seemed to be moving. The birds were all going somewhere, and why not he?

He first cut a good supply of fresh poplar logs at the upper end of the pond and floated them down near the lodge. This took him several days, during which time the spring had been advancing, so, when this task was finished, the frogs were singing in his pond. This was a sure sign of spring and one that should not go unheeded.

The water was pouring through several large breaks in his dam, but what cared he? There was still water enough in the pond to keep the entrances to the lodge under water, but even if it did not, the house could be abandoned, and his family could live in one of the burrows along the bank for a while.

There were Brighteyes and the four frolicsome young beavers to keep him, but the rush of distant waters was in his ears, and he felt just like swimming miles and miles away. Distant waterfalls and rapids were calling to him; deep pools in the river, and wonderful mountain lakes were all waiting for him.

So, one day, when the air was soft and sweet, and the water was getting warm, he slipped away, and Brighteyes knew that she should not see him again until early in September. He was gone to the world of water-wonders, far beyond their limited horizon. She would stay and take care of the babies until his return.

CHAPTER VII

LIFE IN THE WATER WORLD

We have followed the fortunes of Shaggycoat so long that the reader will be interested to know just how he looked, as he swam away into his water world on this warm spring morning.

He was three years old and his weight was already about thirty-five pounds. When he was fully grown, he would weigh fifty-five or possibly sixty pounds. His length was about forty inches, and he would add five or six more to it before he got his full size.

His head and body would then be two feet and three quarters or three feet of his length, and the other foot would be the queerest kind of a paddle shaped tail you ever saw. It was five inches broad at the widest place, and instead of being covered with fur, like the rest of the beaver's body, it was covered with a tough, scaly skin, that gave it quite a fishy look.

It was believed by the ancients that the beaver's tail was fish, and the rest of him was flesh, thus it was lawful to eat the beaver's tail on fast days, when they could not eat meat.

If Shaggycoat had lifted his head out of the water and looked at you as he swam, you would have seen that it was rather small and flat, and that his ears which were small even for the head, nestled down in his fur so that they could hardly be noticed. If you could have examined him near-by, you would have seen that the entrance of each ear was guarded by a fur-covered water pad, which the beaver can close at will and keep the water from his ears. This is very important as he lives so much of the time in the water.

The fact is noticeable all through nature, and particularly in the study of animals, that whenever an animal has need for a peculiar organ, or a peculiar sense, it has been given him.

Sometimes, it is a specially warm coat to shield him from the cold, as in the case of the beaver or otter. Again it will be a long bill, with which to bore in the mud for worms, like that which whistle-wing, the woodcock, possesses; or perhaps it is a stout beak, which can bore into the heart of oak or maple, as the woodpecker does. Wherever there is a peculiar need in nature, there is always a peculiar organism to supply it.

Shaggycoat's fore paws were very short and were held well up under him as he swam. He rarely used them in the water except to hold things in, so they were used more like hands than feet. But his hind legs were long and stout, and they worked away like the screw upon a steamboat, as he moved easily along through the water. His hind feet were also webbed, which gave more resistance, while the legs were set high up on the body, and the stroke was given at an angle, which gave him greater power and sweep. He was altogether a wonderful animal built specially for swimming.

His front teeth were shovel-shaped, two upon each jaw. They came together like wire cutters, and whatever was between them was severed. An alder stick an inch in diameter was severed at a single bite, and small saplings came down in a few seconds.

You may wonder what Shaggycoat saw as he loitered by lake and stream, now skirting a noisy waterfall or turbulent rapids and now loitering in a deep pool. It was a most wonderful world, full of strange creatures and fishes, and the shores of the rivers were frequented by many creatures.

Water is the first necessity with which to sustain life, and lakes and springs are the drinking places of the wild creatures, as well as the home of many of them.

With the fishes that swam in the stream, Shaggycoat was well acquainted, but he rarely molested them and never ate them as the otter did, preferring bark or lily bulbs, for he was a vegetarian.

A beautiful sight that he frequently saw was a lot of salmon jumping a low fall to the pool above. There would be a ripple and a splash, a shower of water would be thrown up, and the sunlight would break into a myriad rainbow hues, and the silver gleam of the fish would glint for a moment in the light. Then there would be a big splash and another rainbow in the pool above and the salmon was gone, and the way was clear for the next one.

Sometimes, Osprey, the great fish-hawk of the Atlantic seaboard (also called in Florida the gray fishing eagle) would come sailing majestically by.

Frequently he uttered his piercing fisherman's cry as he flew. Occasionally, he would almost pause in mid-air, giving just enough motion to his wings to steady himself, then down he would come like a falling star, cleaving the water easily and when he appeared a second or two later, a fish was usually dangling from his talons. Sometimes, it was a sucker, or chub, or if he had been unusually successful, it might be a pickerel or trout.

When he came up, there was always a great shower of water. This when the sunlight played upon it made him look like a bird of wondrous plumage, but, when he had shaken off the water, he was just the plain fish-hawk, though magnificent in flight.

Another smaller fisherman was the queer blue and white kingfisher who caught his fish in his beak instead of his claws. He did not make a great plunge like the fish-hawk when he went fishing, but skimmed along close to the water, and plunged under suddenly and was up again in a second.

He was a comparatively small bird, so had to content himself with small fish.

Then there was Blue-coat, the frog catcher, who could wade easily in a foot of water, his legs being so long and slender. He looked more like a bird on stilts than one on his natural legs, and his beak, which was made especially for frog catching, was long and strong.

He might be seen stepping daintily in some shallow near the shore where there were plenty of lily pads and water grasses. He was very cautious in his movements so as not to scare his victim. He would stand for five minutes on one leg, if he suddenly discovered a frog that he was afraid of scaring, then his long neck would suddenly shoot out. When he drew up his head, a frog would be seen kicking in his bill. He would then hammer the frog on a rock, or spear him with his bill, until life had left him, when he would hide the catch upon the bank and return to his sport.

At dawn and twilight, Shaggycoat frequently saw flocks of ducks and wild geese feeding upon water grasses in sheltered coves. Some of them picked away at things above the water, but others would dive head first and come up bringing a choice bit of grass.

Once a couple of half-grown muskrats were playing in a shallow, chasing each other about in high glee, when the ugly head of a water-snake shot out, and jaws that gripped like death closed upon the young rat's throat. There was a short struggle under water and then a few bubbles floated to the surface and the musquash had been done for. A few moments later Shaggycoat saw the snake swallowing his breakfast on an island in the middle of the stream.

These and other experiences taught the young beaver to always be on the watch and distrust things that seemed strange to him.

The buck drank in the river, and the pretty doe, lank and half starved from suckling her fawn, ate ravenously of the lily pads in the shallow water.

One evening, just at twilight, thoughts of Brighteyes and the baby beavers had so haunted Shaggycoat that he had turned his nose homeward when a peculiar object came round the bend in the stream and on toward the pool where the beaver was playing. It came like a duck, but it was larger than many ducks, and it had two wings, like the fish-hawk, which rose and fell regularly, with a splash of water each time.

There was a buck drinking in the opposite side of the pool from the beaver, and he, too, saw the strange, bright bird that sailed like a duck with wings that splashed in the water. Then a bright flame leaped up, and a roar like thunder resounded across the waters, and rolled away into the distant foothills. The buck snorted, gave a mighty leap, and fell midway in the stream, kicking and thrashing, like a frenzied thing.

All this was strange and terrible to the beaver, who had never heard such thunder, or seen such deadly lightning before, so, without waiting to see more, he fled down stream and hid under the first shelving bank that offered him a hiding-place.

There he lay very still for several hours, but when he ventured out, it was quite dark, and the stranger had gone.

It was man with his deadly "thunderstick," and even the strong buck, with the feet of the wind had been as helpless when it spoke, as his little dappled fawn would have been in the same plight.

Shaggycoat never forgot the scene, or the roar of the "thunderstick," and the scent of the strange creature seemed to linger in his nostrils for days. He had seen enough of this strange and terrible water world for one summer, and would seek his pond, and Brighteyes.

CHAPTER VIII

A BIT OF TRAGEDY

Shaggycoat made his way home in a leisurely manner, stopping a day here and there at some lake or river that pleased his fancy. The home sense had not yet fully mastered him and he still found pleasure in running water, and upon grassy fringed banks.

One morning when he had been upon his homeward journey for about a week, he turned aside to explore a little stream that looked inviting. He intended to return to the river and resume his journey in a few minutes, but the unexpected happened and he did not do as he had intended. He was swimming leisurely in a shallow spot, where the stream was very narrow, when, without any warning, or premonition of danger, he set his foot in a trap. The trap had not been baited but merely set at a narrow point in the stream, in hope that some stray mink or muskrat would blunder into it. It was nothing that Shaggycoat could blame himself for, but merely one of those accidents that befall the most wary animals at times.

The trap was rather light for a beaver, but it had caught him just above the first joint, and held on like a vise. At first Shaggycoat tore about frantically, churning up the water and roiling the stream, seeking by mere strength to free himself, but he soon found that this was in vain. He then tried drowning the trap, but this was equally futile. Next he buried it in the mud but it always came up after him when he sought to steal away. Then he waited for a long time and was quiet, thinking it might let him go of its own accord, but the trap had no such intention.

As the hours wore on, his paw began to swell and pain him, but finally the pain gave place to numbness, and his whole fore leg began to prickle and feel queer. With each hour that passed, a wild terror grew upon Shaggycoat, a terror of he knew not what. The trap gripped him tighter and tighter, and Brighteyes and the young beavers seemed so far away that he despaired of ever seeing them again.

Finally the day passed, the sun set, and the stars came out. The hours of darkness that hold no gloom for a beaver, in which he glories as the other creatures do in day, were at hand; but they held no joy for poor Shaggycoat. Every few minutes he would have a spell of wrenching at the trap, but he was becoming exhausted, although he had thought his strength inexhaustible. At last a desperate thought came to him. It seemed the only way out of the difficulty.

He edged the end of the trap where the chain was, between two stones, then began slowly moving about it in a circle. Occasionally the trap would come loose, then it would be replaced and the twisting process renewed. Finally there was a snap, like the crack of a dry twig, and the bone had been broken. The worst was over. He gnawed away and twisted at the broken paw until it was severed.

Did it hurt? There was no outcry, only the splashing of the water, and a bright trail of blood floated down-stream, and the trap sunk to the bottom to hide the ragged bleeding paw that it still held, while a wiser and a sadder beaver made his way cautiously back to the main stream, licking the ragged stump of his fore paw as he went.

The cold water soon stopped the bleeding and helped to reduce the fever, but Shaggycoat was so spent with the night in the trap that he stopped to rest for two days before resuming his journey homeward.

Just as the sun peeped over the eastern hills on the morning that Shaggycoat freed himself from the trap, a boy of some twelve summers might have been seen hurrying across the fields toward the brook, closely followed by an old black and tan hound. The boy carried a small Stevens Rifle known as the hunter's pet, across his arm, and both boy and dog were excited and eager for the morning's tramp.

In low places where it was moist, the first frost of the season lay heavy upon the grass, and its delicate lace work was still plainly seen on stones and by the brookside. It was a fresh crisp morning, just such a morning as makes one's blood tingle, and whets the appetite.

The birds, as well as the boy, had seen the frost, and the robins were flocking, though most of the summer songsters had already gone.

About half an hour after Shaggycoat left his ragged paw in the trap and swam away, leaving a trail of blood behind him, the boy and dog parted the alder bushes, and came to the spot where the trap had been set.

"By vum, Trixey, something has been in the trap!" exclaimed the boy, as he noted the muddy water and the tracks upon the bank, but he could not see whether there was still anything in the trap because of the silt. He began slowly to haul up the chain, Trixey watching the process eagerly. At last the end of the chain was reached, and the trap dripping water, but containing only the ragged paw, came to the surface.

"Why, Trixey, he's gone!" exclaimed the boy. "It wasn't no muskrat, either. I'll bet it was an otter."

After examining his bloody trophy carefully for a time, the boy reset the trap, and, wrapping the paw in some fern leaves, took it home to prove his story, but it was not until several days afterward when he showed the paw to an old trapper, that he learned that a beaver had been in his trap.

While Shaggycoat is making his way painfully back to his mountain lake, occasionally stopping to favor his freshly amputated paw, let us go back to the lake and see how Brighteyes and the young beavers have been spending the summer.

For the first few days after Shaggycoat's going, it had seemed very lonely without him. He had always been so active, coming and going, that he was greatly missed. But a mother beaver with four lively youngsters to provide for, has many things to think of, so Brighteyes soon found that she was kept quite busy attending to the family and providing food, which had been done before by her mate.

One bright May morning when the air was sweet with the scent of quickening buds, the winds soft with the breath of spring and a throb of joy was in each heart; when beast and bird and man were all glad because the spring had come again, Brighteyes went to the upper end of the pond for some saplings for the supply of bark was low. She left the young beavers in the lodge, where they seemed to be quite safe, but the smell of beaver meat had been tickling the nostrils of the gluttonous wolverine, and he had lingered about the pond all the spring. The beaver lodge had been too hard for him to dig through in midwinter, when it was frozen like a rock, but the sun and winds had drawn the frost from the walls, and now it was no harder than any other mud house.

It was so pleasant outside where everything was singing and springing to the light that Brighteyes stayed longer than she intended, and when she returned and dove into the underground passage, leading to the lodge, she was surprised to find three of the young beavers in the underground channel, as close to the water as they could get. They were very much frightened and did not want to go back into the lodge, so she took them to one of the underground burrows along the bank, and left them there while she reconnoitred.

Brighteyes found to her great surprise that a large hole had been dug in the side of the lodge, and, through the opening, she could see the brown coat of the wolverine. He was eating something, for she could hear the crunching of bones. Presently he heard Brighteyes in the passage and thrust his ugly wolfish head through the hole in the wall. His eye was evil, and his chops were bloody, and something told the mother beaver that the blood was that of her missing young one. Then the wolverine sprang for her through the opening, and she fled precipitately and the friendly water of the pond enfolded her, where she was safe from the glutton.

Brighteyes returned to the remaining youngsters, and after that she guarded them with untiring vigilance. They did not return to the lodge that summer, but lived in the burrows that Shaggycoat had made along the bank. When they got tired of living in one, they moved to another. In this way they were able to shift their base, and still keep the friendly waters of the pond about them.

Although the glutton lingered about the lake for a week or two, he did not again taste beaver meat. So one night he slunk away into the woods in search of some rabbit burrow or fox's hole, from which he might dig out the luckless victims, and the beavers did not see him again. After he had been gone for several days, they came out of hiding and had the freedom of the pond.

When they were large enough, they were taught more of the mysteries of swimming and diving, at which they would play for an hour at a time. In fact they never tired of it.

When they had explored the pond and knew all its windings and its many water recesses, they went upon the bank, but their watchful mother never allowed them to go far ashore. They early learned that the water world was the only safe place for them, and there were dangers to be guarded against even there.

Sometimes, after a swim, they would come upon the bank and sit in the sun to make their toilet. They would rest upon their flat tails, and comb their soft fur with the claws upon their hind paws. It was hard to reach all places upon the body, but they were very patient and combed away persistently. When they had finished, and the sun had dried their coats, they were very sleek and glossy.

One starlight night in September, Brighteyes was swimming home from the upper end of the pond, when she heard a splash in the lake behind her. She quickened her pace, but her pursuer came steadily nearer. There seemed to be something familiar in the sound, so she stopped to investigate. She was now certain of it, so with true female coquetry, she slipped out upon the bank and hid. A moment later Shaggycoat found her there, pretending that she did not know all the time it was he.

Her nose was just as warm, and he was just as glad to see her, as he had been that first night of their tryst. Then the queerest love song that ever broke the starry stillness floated out across the pond. It was a mere murmur, like the sighing of autumn winds in leafless branches. This plaintive love ditty and the weird concert heard in beaver lodges during the summer months and the signal whistle given when a beaver is lost are the three vocal accomplishments of the colony.

CHAPTER IX

STRANGERS AT THE LAKE

After his return to the shimmering Mountain Lake, Shaggycoat allowed himself a few days leisure in which to enjoy the company of Brighteyes and get acquainted with the frolicsome young beavers. They were very shy of him at first, but finally came to know that he was the head of the lodge.

One crisp autumn morning when he went for a swim he discovered that the frost had painted all the trees on the hilltops, and seared the grasses and fronds along the bank of the lake. Then he knew that this idling must cease and hard work upon the dam begin.

The same day just at twilight he went far up-stream to see where he could get material for the dam. It had been badly washed by the spring freshet, and his lake had shrunk to about half its original size. He now planned to rebuild the whole structure, using the two old pines as foundation.

He had slipped out upon the bank, and was busily girdling a poplar, when a strange rhythmic splashing in the stream above fell upon his ear. His first impression was that he had heard something like it before, and somehow the sound filled him with a strange dread. He scrambled quickly to the water and slipped under a friendly screen of pickerel weed where he lay watching and waiting. He could hear the steady splashing plainer now. Then in an instant he remembered the terrifying scene of the drinking buck and the roaring "thunderstick," and his own precipitate flight. This splashing was like that the great duck had made when it came round the bend in the stream. He had hoped to leave that dread thing far behind, and here it was coming to his own home to seek him out, and perhaps destroy them all as it had the buck.

Then it came in sight and he saw that it was larger than many ducks with its two wings rising and falling making a bright splash in the water at each stroke.

Shaggycoat waited to see no more but fled swiftly and noiselessly toward his dilapidated lodge, but he occasionally stopped in a well screened spot to watch and listen for the coming of this monster.

It was not many minutes before he saw it enter the lake, and then he knew that his retreat had been discovered by the most subtle and destructive of all his foes, man.

Shaggycoat fled to the lodge and told Brighteyes all that he had seen and heard, and they counseled together as to what course to pursue.

Brighteyes was for fleeing at once, but Shaggycoat could not tear himself away from this spot that he had selected so carefully and the dam that had cost him so much labor, so he counseled waiting another day. They could be very wary and never show themselves except by night and if they kept to the burrows that he had dug along the bank, he felt quite sure that the stranger could not get at them, so he went back to watch these invaders of his stronghold, while Brighteyes hid the young beavers in the largest of the burrows near the dam. Although the water was low in the lake, it was deep here, and she felt quite secure.

The two canoeists never imagined as they paddled down the lake, that a wary beaver was keeping just so far ahead of them, swimming from stump to overhanging bank and watching their every movement. When they hauled their canoe ashore and made a camp-fire, they little suspected that they were camping within fifty feet of the underground burrow of the beaver.

While they were cooking supper a flock of ducks came sailing over and three of their number alighted in the lake to feed upon water grass. Then Shaggycoat saw one of the strangers pick up the black stick that had spoken so loudly to the buck on the river bank a few days before. He felt a strong impulse to flee but there was a strange fascination about it all and he wanted to see what happened.

While he was still wondering which was the better course to pursue, the "thunderstick" spoke, and its echo rolled along the lake and was thrown from hillside to hillside, again and again. It seemed to Shaggycoat that his quiet lake had suddenly become the abode of thunder and lightning. He waited to see no more but fled to the burrow, where he found Brighteyes and the young beavers trembling with fright.

The same evening, an hour or two later, Shaggycoat heard an ominous whack, whack, whack upon his dam. It reminded him so forcibly of the pounding that they heard in the old Beaver City, before he and his grandfather had fled that he was filled with dismay. Was his own small dam and the lodge that he had reared with so much labor to be destroyed just as the old Beaver City had been, and he and Brighteyes slain?

The following day the strangers made very free with the beaver's pond, or at least Shaggycoat thought so, as he watched them covertly from a bunch of alders that grew partly in the water.

What right had they to go paddling about in their great red duck just as though they owned his lake?

They stopped at the island and examined the dilapidated lodge critically, but they took still greater liberties for they finally dug a hole in the side of the house and looked inside.

They were much interested in the beaver's dwelling and seemed to be trying to find out all about him.

It angered Shaggycoat extremely to see all these liberties taken with his possessions but what could he do against the strangers with a "thunderstick" that could kill a tall buck; so he discreetly kept out of sight, knowing that he could repair the house in a few minutes if they would only go away and leave the lake to its rightful owners.

At night the strangers again killed a duck with the "thunderstick" and drawing their canoe upon the bank made a fire.

Shaggycoat determined to go nearer to them that night and see if he could discover what kind of creatures they were. He had just left the burrow upon his hazardous expedition when he heard a pounding that reminded him of the pounding on the ice when the trappers had come and cut holes about their lodges. It could not be that they were cutting holes in the ice now, for there was no ice, but the steady pounding filled him with dread.

Again Brighteyes counseled that they flee at once leaving all to the strangers, but Shaggycoat would not go.

When the pounding ceased and the usual quiet reigned, for there was always the sighing of the wind, or perhaps the hooting of an owl, he crept cautiously forth to see what these meddlesome creatures had been doing.

The first thing he discovered alarmed him extremely. The water was falling and there was a great hole in his dam. Why not flee at once? But where? Had not he and his grandfather fled for days and weeks, and the strangers had found him out at last. They would discover him again if he fled.

But the rapidity with which the water was falling alarmed him more than even the thought of these dread strangers. If it should fall below the mouth of their burrow, their enemies could get them. The break in the dam must be repaired at once, so he hurried back to the burrow to tell his mate and they set to work.

First they sought to stem the flow of water temporarily, until they could do it thoroughly, so they swam up the lake fifteen or twenty rods and going ashore gathered each an armful of weeds and cat-tails. These they carried to the dam, holding them in their arms and swimming in a more upright position than usual.

They threw the weeds into the break, but the swift current swept them away in a very few seconds. This would not do; they must try something more substantial, so Shaggycoat went ashore and cut strong stakes and stuck them in the mud at either end of the break. Then they cut a dozen alder bushes and laid them across, allowing the stakes to hold them at either end. The current could not sweep this away, but the water still flowed freely through the bushes and something finer was now needed.

They again swam up the lake and returned with their arms full of weeds. These they wove in and out among the alder bushes, but the work was not complete until they had brought mud and plastered it solid. When this had been done, the flow of water was effectually stopped.

Then Shaggycoat sat upon his broad tail and viewed their work critically. He had become so absorbed in repairing the dam that he had for the moment forgotten the strangers who had caused him this trouble.

He was wondering whether they had better bring more mud when a strong puff of wind filled his nostrils with a strange repugnant scent. It sent a shiver of dread through him, and caused the long hairs to rise upon his neck. Where had he smelled that before? Somewhere he had caught such a scent, and the remembrance of it was not pleasant.

Then it came back to him. It was at the old Beaver City when the trappers were chopping holes in the ice and destroying its inhabitants. The trap also into which he had stepped the summer before had been strong with the same odor. Then the beaver's eyes grew big with wonder and fright, for there in the tree above him, not fifty feet away, he saw one of the dreaded strangers watching him. With a resounding slap his tail smote the water and a second later, only a ripple showed where the beaver had disappeared.

The following morning the meddlesome strangers loaded their belongings into the great duck, carried it around the end of the dam and paddled away down stream.

It was with great joy that Shaggycoat observed from his place of hiding, these movements on their part. But he thought they might be trying to fool him, so he followed at a distance.

When he had seen them round a bend in the stream nearly a mile from the dam, he concluded that their leaving was no sham, and went back to his lake, well pleased with the turn of affairs.

He and Brighteyes and another pair of beavers, who had returned with him from his summer ramble, began work on the dam and by the time the first freeze came, it was strong and symmetrical and higher and longer than it had been before. This made the water set back and several families of musquash, who had built along the shore of the lake, were drowned out, and obliged to gather new supplies of winter edibles.

This angered the muskrat families who revenged themselves on the beavers in a way they did not like.

In the morning, when the builders left off working on the dam, it would be in good shape, but by twilight it would be leaking badly.

Examination showed many holes tunneled through the mud, which made the dam leak. For several days Shaggycoat could not discover who was molesting his dam, but he finally set a watchman, and the destroyers were caught in the act. After that whenever a muskrat was seen anywhere near the dam, he was rudely hurried to another part of the lake. When the dam had been repaired, the lodge was attended to, but this winter there were two lodges on the island instead of one.

The forest was now entirely denuded and the naked arms of maple and poplar swayed fitfully in the rude gusts of the boisterous early winter wind. In its mad careering down the aisles of the pathetic forest, it caught up the dead leaves and whirled them about gleefully.

Summer had had its day, and November must now have its inning.

Down from the distant foothills which were now sere and brown, came a shuffling, shambling black figure, closely followed by two little shuffling, shambling figures. It was evident that more strangers were coming to the beavers' lake.

They sniffed at the bushes, and poked under the dead leaves inquisitively as they came. Whenever they discovered nuts, they ate them greedily. These figures were not agile, like most of the denizens of the woods, but rather clumsy. Whenever they planted their large paws (which were armed with massive claws) upon a twig, it crunched under the weight with a muffled sound.

It did not snap as it would have done under the hoof of a deer or crack as under the hoof of a moose, but it simply crunched.

The figures did not go stealthily like the cat family or furtively like a fox, but there was a certain cunning in their manner, which was more shrewd than suspicious.

Whenever they crowded through heavy underbrush, they occasionally left long black hairs, which hunters would at once identify, as coming from the warm winter coat of Bruin.

An old mother bear and two cubs were making their way down to the beavers' lake, which they had seen from the foothills.

The old bear was leading the way as was her wont, and the cubs were following like dutiful children.

There were no sheepfolds in this wilderness so far from the haunts of man, and, as for pig, the old bear had not tasted it since early in the spring. Some instinct or intuition told her that the beautiful forest lake was the work of a beaver, and if their houses had not been frozen up too hard, they might be broken into and made to pay toll to the family of Bruin.

So the errand of these strangers boded no good for Shaggycoat and his household.

The old bear and the two cubs came out upon the lake just at the dam, and as there was a fresh wind blowing from up-stream, beaver scent was strong.

Then the countenance of the old bear, which was usually droll and good natured, became cunning and eager with the thought of beaver meat.

The conical beaver houses were out on an island some distance from the shore so the old bear tried the ice and found that it held. Then she went slipping and sliding over the smooth surface to the island, closely followed by the cubs.

She walked about the larger of the two lodges several times before deciding what to do, then reared upon her hind legs and peeped in at the vent. There, almost within reach of her paw, were four or five sleek beavers.

The sight of meat so near at hand caused the old bear to forget her cunning and she thrust one of her powerful forearms in at the vent reaching wildly for the beavers. Then what a scrambling there was for both the front and back door of the lodge, as the astonished and terrified beavers made their escape.

Seeing that this tactic was useless, Bruin withdrew her paw, and again peeped in, but the beaver house was quite empty.

Even with her strong arms, she could not tear off the top of the lodge which was frozen hard as stone.

After spending two days in futile efforts to get at the beavers, the three bears shambled off through the wood in search of winter quarters.

They were not long in finding a fallen tree with a heavy top which made a good covering, so they crawled in and went to sleep. Soon the heavy snow-storms covered them up snug and warm, and the only evidence that the tree-top was the home of three bears, was a small hole melted in the snow where the breath of the three sleepers thawed it. This was their chimney through which their warm breath would ascend until spring.

When the strong forearm of the old bear, with its powerful claws, had raked the beavers' lodge in search of supper, Shaggycoat and his family had not fully understood the intruder's motive, although they knew quite well that it was sinister.

The following summer, however, during his annual ramble, Shaggycoat learned all about the bears' fondness for the beaver, and this bit of knowledge increased his fear of the bear family.

He had frequently seen Bruin watching the fish in some deep pool and trying whenever they came to the surface to sweep one out on the land with his paw, but one day he discovered a bear watching something else in the water.

Shaggycoat could not see anything to watch, but he did notice an occasional bubble coming to the surface. This was what interested the bear.

Presently Bruin dove head first into the water and after remaining down for several seconds came blowing and puffing to the surface, bringing a half drowned beaver in his jaws. If anything more was needed to add to the unfortunate beaver's trouble, it was that one of his forepaws was firmly held in a trap. The bear had evidently discovered the beaver in a trap, and had driven him to the bottom. He laid his unfortunate victim down and with one blow of his strong paw broke the beaver's neck.

This was enough for Shaggycoat and he fled like a hunted thing, and after that day he always kept as much water between himself and the bear family as possible.

CHAPTER X

A TROUBLESOME FELLOW

The first time that Shaggycoat saw the brown fisherman, he came sliding over the surface of the beavers' pond, and the manner of his coming both astonished and angered Shaggycoat.

The thing that astonished him was to see the otter slide, and he was angry, because the stranger acted just as though the pond belonged to him and Shaggycoat knew that it was his own. Had he not spent days and weeks searching in the wilderness for a spot where he could make his home and had not he and Brighteyes built the dam that flowed the meadow? It was all his and the manner of this merry stranger made him furious.

He would show him who was master here, so the beaver began swimming rapidly about under the ice, trying vainly to find an escape to the outer air. But Jack Frost had shut down a transparent ice window over the pond the night before, and, although Shaggycoat could still see the sky and the trees along the shore, yet the outer world would not be his again until spring. He could find an airhole by going up-stream two or three miles to some rapids, but the return trip overland was not inviting, for he, like other beavers, was a poor pedestrian and would not go any long distance except by water. So true is this of the beaver, that one naturalist says he may be kept a prisoner in a certain portion of a stream, simply by placing wire netting across the current and running it inland for a hundred feet in either direction. A beaver so held between two wire fences at right angles to the stream, will spend several days in captivity before he will venture around the end of the fence to freedom.

It was out of the question for Shaggycoat to go two miles up-stream and think of returning overland merely to fight, so he gave up the plan and amused himself by watching the otter.

He had never seen any one so agile before and he would have been amused at the otter's pranks, had it not been upon his own particular pond.

The otter would go up the bank where it was steep and give three or four great jumps. When he struck the surface ice, he would double his fore legs up so that they lay along his sides, and slide across the ice on his breast, trailing his hind legs.

Then he would scramble up the opposite bank and repeat the performance, carrying him nearly back to the other side. Shaggycoat thought he had never seen anything quite so interesting in his life and he swam about under the ice watching his visitor.

Finally in one of his slides the otter passed over the spot where Shaggycoat was and saw him for the first time.

He could not stop in his slide in time to pay his compliments to the beaver, but he soon came slipping and sliding back and glared down at the owner of the pond showing a set of teeth, almost as good as the beaver's own.

Shaggycoat glared back at him and they both knew the fight would come some other day.

The otter seemed to say by his looks, "Come up here and I will shake you out of that drab coat," and the beaver's countenance replied, "You just come down here and I'll drown you and then tear you to pieces just to see what your brown coat is made of."

Shaggycoat saw a great deal of the otter on these crisp, clear days, before the ice became clouded, and his coming and going always made the beaver uneasy.

Sometimes this playful coaster would slide the entire length of the pond, going half a mile in two or three minutes. He would stick his sharp claws into the ice and give two or three bounds, then he would slide a long distance.

The momentum that he got from the springs would usually carry him seventy-five or a hundred yards.

Shaggycoat thought it must be great sport, but the coaster should play upon his own pond, if he had one, and leave other people's undisturbed.

Finally a great fall of snow spread a soft, white, impenetrable blanket over the ice, and the beaver saw no more of his enemy until spring.

At last with their golden key the sun-beams unlocked the ice door over the lake and the denizens of beaver city were again free to go and come in the outer world. Then Shaggycoat swam a mile or so up-stream to look for elderberry wood. There was something in the pungent acid sap of the elderberry that he craved after the inactive life of winter. This was his spring medicine, a tonic that the beaver always seeks if he can find it, when the first great thaw opens the ice in the river.

He also was fond of the sweet maple sap and stopped to girdle a small soft maple on the way. He would remember that maple and come again. The sap would run freely during the day and freeze at night and in the morning the ice would be covered with syrup, white, transparent, and sweet as honey. This was a primitive sugar-making in which the beaver indulged.

He had satisfied his spring craving for both sweet and sour with maple and elder sap and was swimming leisurely down-stream toward his lake when he heard a sound on shore. Something was coming through the woods, for he heard the snow crackling. Shaggycoat kept very still and watched and listened. Nearer and nearer the sounds came and presently he saw the otter coming with long jumps, breaking the crust at every spring. They discovered each other almost at the same instant and the otter was all fight in a second. The fur stood up on his neck, his eyes snapped, and his lips parted showing a white, gleaming set of teeth.

He made straight for the beaver, covering the snow with great jumps and Shaggycoat saw that his best course was to meet his enemy in the water. On land he would be no match for so agile a foe. So he swam in mid-stream and clambered upon a low rock and waited for the attack. This was the hour for which he had longed all through the winter months, but now that it was at hand, he almost wished that he was back in his snug house on the lake. The otter was a third larger than he, and he swam so easily and his every motion was so quick and strong that the beaver feared him even before he had found how good a fighter he was.

He began by swimming about the rock several times, snapping at his adversary at every chance. This necessitated Shaggycoat's turning very fast and as he was not as quick as his foe, he got his tail nipped twice almost before he knew it. Then he concluded the rock was no place for him so made a clumsy spring for the otter's back. But when he fell in the water with a great splash, the otter was not where he had been a second before, but was glaring at the beaver from the rock which he had reached in some unaccountable manner.

While Shaggycoat was still wondering what to do next, the otter took matters into his own hands, by jumping squarely upon the beaver's back, and setting his teeth into his neck. It would have been a sorry day for poor Shaggycoat had not a projecting rock been near by, under which he plunged, scraping off his enemy, and thus saving his neck from being badly chewed, if not broken. He was getting decidedly the worst of it, so when the otter went back to the rock, Shaggycoat swam out from his hiding-place, and started for the lake at his best speed with his foe in hot pursuit.

What a swim that was and how they churned up the water in that running fight back to the lake. The beaver with his strong hind legs working desperately, doubling, twisting, and turning, snapping at his enemy whenever that agile fellow gave him a chance, and the otter gliding with swift, strong strokes, swimming over and under the beaver and punishing him at every turn. Foam and blood flecked the water and a line of bubbles marked their progress.

It seemed to Shaggycoat that his stronghold toward which he was retreating, fighting off his heavy foe so valiantly, was miles away, but at last, to his great joy, it was reached, and there, at the upper end of the lake was Brighteyes, licking at the maple stump that he had girdled that morning. Like a faithful helpmate she flew to his relief, and the otter, seeing that he had two beavers to fight instead of one, gave up the chase and swam away.

It is doubtful if he would have fought a female beaver, for there is a certain chivalry shown the sex, even in the woods.

The next otter that Shaggycoat saw was much smaller than his enemy and he at once concluded that it was a female, which proved to be the case. She was lying upon a rock in mid-stream, watching the water closely. Her intense manner at once attracted the beaver's attention, so he kept quiet and watched just to find out what she was doing.

Presently she sprang from the rock like a flash and swam down-stream with a rapidity that fairly took Shaggycoat's breath away, good swimmer that he was. But he was still more astonished, when a second later she struck out for the shore bearing a large fish in her jaws. The fish was giving a few last feeble flops with its tail.

What she wanted with the nasty fish, Shaggycoat could not imagine, so he kept still and watched. She lay down upon the sand, and holding the fish down with one paw, began tearing it to pieces and eating it. She had not been long at work when Shaggycoat noticed two otter pups, that had previously escaped his attention, playing in the sand near the old otter. They were as playful as kittens and were rolling and tumbling about having a merry time. When the old otter had finished her fish, she called the youngsters to her, and lying down upon the sand, gave them their own supper, which was neither flesh nor fish.

When they were satisfied, she tried to coax them into the water. She would plunge in herself, and then face about and stand pleading with them, but they were afraid and would not venture in. Finally, one a little bolder than the other, came to the water's edge, and dipped his paw in it, but evidently did not like it, for he went back on the bank. Then the old otter resorted to a strange stratagem, and got her way as mothers will.

She lay down upon the sand and romped and rolled with her pups, tumbling them over and over. Finally at the height of the play, they were coaxed upon her back, when she slipped quickly into the stream, where she tumbled them off, and left them kicking and sputtering. A moment later they scrambled out looking like drowned rats. But the lesson that she had sought to teach them had been learned. They had discovered that the water did them no harm and before the shades of night had fallen and the stars appeared, they were playing in the stream of their own accord.

All this amused Shaggycoat so much that he forgot to be angry with the old otter, and finally went away to look for his own supper of poplar bark.

Later in the summer, he did really meet his enemy face to face, but under such strange conditions that the beaver never forgot the incident.

He was swimming rapidly down-stream on the return trip to Brighteyes and his own forest lake. There were other lakes in the wilderness that he visited each summer during his long rambles but none quite like his, so he was hastening in the autumn twilight, for he knew that in two or three days he would again be at home.

Suddenly, as he rounded a sharp bend in the stream, he came upon his enemy close at hand. The otter seemed to be engaged in wrestling with something in the water. He was near shore and making quite a splash.

All of the old fury came back to Shaggycoat. This was the fellow who had so punished him on that memorable day, but Shaggycoat was now larger and stronger than he had been the year before. He felt that he was a match for the otter. He would punish him now so that he would never dare to slide upon his pond again.

Shaggycoat started forward noiselessly to take his enemy by surprise and had gotten within twenty yards before the otter saw him and then that bold fellow seemed greatly frightened. He plunged about frantically and churned up the water, roiling the stream. Then it was that Shaggycoat noticed something strange which sent the fur up on his neck and all along his back and recalled sensations that were anything but pleasant. When the otter reared and plunged, the beaver saw that his forepaw was firmly held in the cruel thing that had caught him the year before.

Now was his time. The trap would hold the otter tight and he would punish him. Again the otter reared and plunged, and a new possibility came to Shaggycoat. Perhaps there were more traps all about them. Maybe there was one right under his paws this very minute. His fury at his enemy gave way to fear for his own safety and he fled precipitately not even waiting to see if his enemy got free. As he fled, the terror of traps grew upon him, so that for miles he did not dare to touch his paws on the bottom of the stream.

At last, weary and exhausted, he crawled under an overhanging bank and slept, and in sleep forgot the fear that had pursued him all through the night. But his enemy never troubled him again, either upon the streams that he frequented in summer, or on his own forest lake in winter.

CHAPTER XI

A BANK BEAVER

When Shaggycoat returned from his second summer's ramble, he brought home with him a large good natured beaver whom we will call Brownie.

This newcomer to the valley was a third larger than Shaggycoat, and lighter colored. The long hairs in his glossy coat were light brown, while his under fur was a drab. His tail was also larger and longer than that of his host.

Brownie turned out to be what is called a bank beaver. In France all the beavers are bank beavers; in America they were all house beavers originally, but they have been so crowded and hunted from their native haunts by trappers and frontiersmen, that many of them have become bank beavers; probably because this mode of life is less conspicuous, and leaves them better protected from the attacks of man, but they are a more easy prey to their natural enemies, and to starvation in the winter.

Naturalists have quarreled and disputed as scientists will, as to whether the bank beaver in America is a separate specie, or merely the house beaver, who has adopted the methods and manners of the bank beaver.

I am inclined to the latter view, as birds, animals, and even plants will modify their mode of life to suit changing conditions.

At first Shaggycoat liked Brownie very much. He was so good natured and playful that he made a pleasant companion, on the return trip home, but, when work upon the dam began, and he was invited to put his strong muscles in play, he demurred. There was no need of building a dam he thought. Why not be content with a hole in the bank, and then there would be no need of cutting these great trees, and tugging and hauling on logs and stones. Small trees furnished just as good bark as large ones, and were much easier to cut. But Shaggycoat did not like this lazy manner of living, besides he did not think it safe. When day after day Brownie refused to help on the dam, he flew into a rage with so lazy a fellow, and gave Brownie such a severe trouncing that he never dared show himself about the lake afterward, so he went a mile or so down stream, and set up housekeeping for himself. But there was not much house about it, for his home was merely a deserted otter's den, although he considered it quite adequate.

One naturalist asserts that the bank beaver in America is a forlorn, sorrowful fellow, who has been disappointed in love, and has to go through life without a mate; while another avers that he is a drone who will not labor, and so is driven from the colony.

Brownie certainly was a drone, and perhaps he had left his little mud love token along the watercourse that autumn, and it had remained unopened, but certainly his was a lonely life.

He took up his abode about a mile below the dam, and although they sometimes saw him watching them from a distance, he never dared again trespass on the premises of these more ambitious beavers.

His burrow was located where the river was deep so that he might be well protected from the waterside. He could not lay up a large supply of wood for food as the house beaver did, but he managed to secure considerable under roots and stones along the shore. Some of this the current carried down stream, and his stock ran short before spring.

Perhaps he thought of his snugly housed cousins on cold winter days and nights, as he nestled alone in his comfortless burrow. In the beaver houses, the warmth of several bodies, and the breath from many nostrils, kept the temperature quite comfortable, but lonely Brownie had to be his own bedfellow, and what warmth there was came from his own body, and warming one's self with one's own heat is rather a forlorn task.

Also when his supply of bark ran low, and he had to gnaw upon tree roots to keep the breath of life in his body, he remembered the house beaver's generous supply of wood.

If the winter was not too severe, the stream might be open for a while at the rapids near by, when he could replenish his store, but, floundering about in the deep snow in midwinter, leaving telltale tracks at every step, and an unmistakable beaver scent, was hazardous business. There were many creatures in the wilderness who were fiercer and stronger than the harmless beaver, and they all loved beaver meat.

As we have already seen, the bear would prowl about in beaver land, just before denning up, for a last smack of blood. The wildcat and the lynx were about as fond of beaver as of fish and they could watch for both at the same time, which made it doubly interesting. The sneaking wolverine also considered the beaver his particular titbit.

For all of these reasons Brownie would go hungry for several meals before he would venture outside to replenish his store of bark.

One evening late in November, he was leaving his burrow to go ashore and do some wood cutting when just at the entrance a premonition of danger came upon him. That peculiar sense of danger that many animals have told him that something was wrong. I have known several cases where dogs had premonitions of coming disaster in the family, and it was probably this instinctive power that told Brownie that something was waiting for him at the mouth of his burrow, so he just poked the tip of his nose out, to see what it was that made him so uncomfortable.

Quick as a flash a mighty paw armed with a raking set of claws, struck him a stunning blow in the nose. He had just sense enough left to wriggle back a few feet into the burrow, and keep quiet.

Although his nose was bleeding profusely and he had been severely stunned, in a few seconds he recovered, for without doctors, or medicine, the wild creatures have a way of recovering rapidly from any hurt.

From the strong bear scent that penetrated his burrow, Brownie knew that his enemy was a bear, even before Bruin reached his strong arm in and tried to poke him out. But he had no mind to be poked, so he wriggled out of reach and was glad that he had escaped so easily. The bear hung about the spot for a day or two, often watching cat-like at the hole. Sometimes he would go back into the woods, hoping to entrap the beaver into coming out, but Brownie had no desire to become further acquainted with the ugly fellow and so stayed in, although this two days' imprisonment hindered his wood cutting.

The next watcher at his front door was the mean, sneaking wolverine, who kept him a prisoner for two or three days more. This enemy was even more to be dreaded than the bear, for he would have dug the beaver out if the mouth of his burrow had not been so far under water. He did start to dig him out from the bank above, running a shaft down to strike the beaver den. He would have found the burrow without a doubt, but a hard freeze put a stop to his digging so he left the bank beaver and went up to the dam to try his luck with the house beavers.

All these things made Brownie's supply of wood much smaller than it should have been. But the trouble was not there. He should have been more provident, and worked earlier in the autumn when he had a chance.

Finally the ice door was shut down over lake and stream, and there was no more going out for the beaver family.

Now Brownie was unwise again, for he did not guard his store carefully, but ate greedily without a thought of how long the winter before him might be.

By the time the great January thaw came he had entirely exhausted his supply of bark and had gnawed all the tree roots that he could reach under the ice.

He would have famished in a few days more had not the great thaw opened an airhole in the ice, through which he escaped into the adjacent woods. He knew that this was hazardous, but hunger impelled him and hunger is a mighty argument. For about a week all went well and he was congratulating himself upon his good fortune, and had about concluded that he had been too cautious, when the unexpected happened. This night he went forth as usual to cut sapling for his supper but did not return.

Just what happened I shall not tell, but we will follow his tracks in the snow and see if we can guess.

For three or four rods we can see where he floundered along to a clump of bushes, and here there are four ragged stumps and near by three small poplars lying in the snow. Then here are the marks of brush being dragged along on the snow to the burrow. Then there is a second beaver track leading back to the fallen poplars, and here is another track coming from down-stream and following beside the beaver track. This track shows four large paw prints in a bunch and the creature did not trot but hopped like a rabbit.

Now he has stopped, for the paw prints are spread out as though he stood watching and listening. See where the fur on his belly brushed the snow as he crept forward. Now he is crouching low, the belly mark on the snow is plainer. What a break in the track is this. Three great jumps, each measuring ten feet, and here are other tracks of the same kind coming from two directions.

See how the snow is tramped and blurred. Ah, there is where the hunter and hunted met, and the pale winter moon and the gleaming stars know what happened.

There are still a few small drops of blood, and eager tongues have licked up many more, for the snow is blotted and streaked with these tongue marks. Here and there are brown hairs that tell their pathetic story to the woodsman who can see it all in the tracks as well as though it had happened before his own eyes.

The unfortunate wood-cutter had fallen a victim to one of those ferocious lynx bands, that range the woods in extreme winters when hunger drives them to hunt in company. It had been cleverly done as things are, in the woods. One of the company had come up the stream and cut off the beaver's chance of escape to his burrow. He had then followed on the fresh track to the poplars where the band had closed in on their unfortunate prey.

Only the uncanny night knows how pitiful was the cry from the terrified and agonized beaver as these three furies hurled themselves upon him and in fewer seconds than it takes to tell it, tore him to shreds.

CHAPTER XII

THE BUILDERS

When the tardy spring at last came to Beaver City, it was with a rush.

On the first day of March the snow was three feet deep in the woods along the foothills, and two feet upon the smooth surface of the beavers' lake. By the tenth of the month, one might search long to find even a small snow-bank along the north side of the woods, or behind some protecting boulder.

The wind, the rain, and the sun had all combined to bring about this marvelous change.

For three days "it had rained suds," as the country people say, and then a merry south wind had blown across the fog-covered snow-banks.

All the little streams hastening down the mountainside became raging torrents, and the larger stream emptying into Beaver Lake, fairly went mad.

In a single night it rose several feet, breaking up the ice, and tossing it about as a child might his toys.

In some places the great gleaming cakes were shouldered out upon the shore, and piled up in massive blockhouses. In other places they jammed, making a very good ice dam across the stream. Then the water would set back until it felt strong enough to cope with the ice, when it would sweep the dam away and go thundering down-stream tossing the ice about and sweeping all before it.

It was such a jam as this that dammed the water just above Beaver Lake, holding it until the stream foamed and raged like an infuriated monster. Then with a roar like thunder it burst through. Thousands of tons of ice accumulated and piled up mountains high. The ice in the lake was broken up like glass, and the mighty weight of all these contending forces, pressed continually upon the beaver's strong dam.

For a while the sturdy old pines which were the backbone of the structure held, but finally, creaking, groaning and snapping, they were wrenched from their places, and with a great rush the beaver dam went out. Then hundreds of grating, grinding, thundering cakes of ice followed after the rushing waters.

When the ice jam struck the upper end of the island where the lodges were, Shaggycoat knew that it was no place for him and his family, so led a precipitate flight for terra firma. They were fortunate enough to find an open place between the cakes of ice at the lower end of the island, and all escaped into the alder bushes along the shore.

But they did not feel safe out in the open, with no house to flee to, so as soon as the ice went out and the water fell, they went back to the burrows.

When the spring freshet had passed, even the entrances to these strongholds were left high and dry, and the broad area that had been their lake looked very much as it had the first time Shaggycoat saw it.

It would never do to leave the female beavers and the youngsters in this unprotected way while the males were off for their summer ramble, so they constructed a brush and stone dam that should flow a small area, and make the lodges again tenable. This was done by weighting down the brush with heavy stones, letting the butts of the bushes point down-stream. This structure was finally covered with sods and mud, making a good temporary dam.

When Shaggycoat returned from his third summer of rambling in distant lakes and streams he brought back three sturdy pairs of beaver, whom he had invited to share his pleasant valley.

There was a definite plan in the wise head of our beaver, for the furtherance of which he needed more help than his small colony now afforded.

When the water had stood six feet deep in the bed of the stream, where the old pines had been, it had flowed the lowlands from foothill to foothill, and had stretched away up-stream until it was lost in the distance. The picture of this silvern lake, sparkling and shimmering in the bright spring sunlight, had captivated Shaggycoat, who had seen it all from a knoll on shore. The old dam and the old lake, covering about half this territory, would never do for him again. There must be a dam built that would flow all this country, and he would be the builder.

When the water had fallen, he had gone over the meadows, noting by the watermark upon trees and bushes just how his lake would extend, and how deep the water would be in certain places. The flood had surveyed the meadows for him, and all he had to do was to look about.

He had noticed when the water stood six feet deep in the channel, that the width of the stream where the dam would be placed was about one hundred and fifty feet, so this would be the length of his dam.

Although it was still early in the fall, no time was lost. The task before them was seemingly almost impossible for such small creatures.

Ten eager wood-cutters were sent up-stream about a mile to a poplar grove, where they began felling trees of from six to twelve inches in diameter. These were cut into logs about three feet in length, and tumbled into the stream. When it became choked or the sticks lodged along the shore, two or three beavers were detailed to act as river-men, so they pushed and pulled, swimming about among the logs until the channel was free again. Several two-year-olds worked industriously, gathering flood wood that had lodged upon the meadows, after the spring freshet. This was also pushed into the water and started down-stream.

On the site of the new dam, Shaggycoat and Brighteyes, with one other old beaver, were working away with might and main, straightening out the remains of the old dam, and getting the foundations of the new structure ready.

Soon the poplar logs came floating down to the waiting builders. Here they were seized by strong paws, and carried upon sturdy backs to their place, in the cobwork dam.

For the first two feet, the dam would be built three tiers wide. This would make the thickness at the base about ten feet. The cracks between the logs were plastered up with sods and mud or if it seemed to call for more weight stones were occasionally used.

Soon the logs and drift-wood began to come down faster than the three at the dam could handle it for it must be laid nicely, and often one stick was placed in several positions before it suited. It would never do to have any of this building material go down-stream so two or three of the cutting gang were shifted to the dam, and the work went on.

Whenever the logs in the stream grew scarce, some of the workers at the dam went back to cutting logs. When the logs in the current jammed, river-men were quickly hurried to loosen them. There was one accident that marred the pleasure of dam-building and made the day memorable in the colony. This did not stop the work, for these things happen in the woods and the waters, where they get used to the unexpected.

One of Shaggycoat's first litter, who was now a sturdy beaver of three summers, was felling a poplar larger than most of the trees which they were using.

He was a famous wood-cutter, and wanted to distinguish himself by cutting a large tree. He had worked away all night, and when the others stopped at daylight his tree was not yet down so he stayed to finish it, but, as the morning hours went by and he did not return to the lodge, Shaggycoat went in search of him.

He found him lying at the stump of the fallen tree with his skull crushed. He had evidently tried to take one more bite at the tottering tree, when a prudent beaver would have stopped, and his head had been crushed between the stump and the falling trunk.

This is an accident that sometimes occurs, although as a whole these little wood-cutters are very cautious.

There was nothing to do in this case but leave the unfortunate victim where he had fallen, but the tree was never used.

When the dam was two feet high, it was narrowed to two tiers of logs. Then they could get on faster, but the higher it went, the longer it had to be carried out at the ends. As the water set back it was much easier to float the logs down.

The three tiers of logs at the bottom of the dam were occasionally tied together by putting on a log ten feet long that would lie across all three tiers. The cutting and placing of such a stick would take the combined strength of four or five beavers.

When this long stick was ready, extra help was summoned and it was rolled into the stream.

About the same tactics were used in placing it in the dam, but, when it was once placed, it tied the three tiers of logs firmly together.

When the water rose too high above the dam, a small opening would be made just large enough to keep it a little below the working line.

Thus, night after night they worked, felling trees, floating down logs, and placing them, bringing mud and sods, and slowly moulding the whole into a strong symmetrical structure.

Men would have required skilful engineers with levels and other instruments and much figuring before the work had been begun, but not so the beaver. The spring freshet had done the surveying to Shaggycoat's entire satisfaction, and the small difficulties were overcome as fast as they arose by their remarkable building genius.

I do not suppose the beaver knew the old maxim that "water seeks its level," but they always acted as though they did, and were continually profiting by the fact.

Before the first of December, the dam was completed, at least for that year. This kind of a dam could be enlarged at any time, as the needs of Beaver City grew.

Then the lodges had to be attended to. The new level of water had flooded the lower story of the old lodge on the island, so the top was ripped off, and a new floor laid and another story was added.

While the old lodges were being repaired, four new houses went up, so that the colony now numbered seven lodges, while the lake stretched back through the lowlands for more than a mile.

Along the newly formed shores, alder bushes now stood deep in the water. When it had frozen over, and fresh bark could not longer be gotten, these bushes would be remembered.

At last the great freeze came; the glass door was shut down over the lake, and Jack Frost installed as doorkeeper until spring-time.

But what cared the beaver? Their lodges were now frozen like adamant, and the new dam was equal to the task put upon it. There were cords of poplar logs stored along the dam under the water, and thrust into the mud about the lodges, so they could eat and sleep while the winter months went by. They had done their work well, and this was their reward.

CHAPTER XIII

BEAVER JOE

Joe Dubois, or Beaver Joe, as he was known to the Factor and his fellow woodsmen, was the most successful trapper who had ever baited steel jaws for the Hudson Bay Company in all its long history of two hundred and twenty-five years. Not in all the howling wilderness from the Great Lakes to the mouth of the Mackenzie, and from Labrador to the Selkirks, was there another who brought in such packs of skins.

Joe's fellow trappers said that mink and muskrat would play tag on the pans of his traps just for fun, and that the beaver loved Joe's body scent on the trap, better than its own castor, an oily substance taken from the beaver and nearly always used in baiting the trap.

Joe was a half-breed, his father being a Frenchman and his mother an Indian girl. It was his father who had given him the nickname of Beaver Joe, but his mother called him by a long Indian name, which I can neither spell nor pronounce, but it signified man of many traps.

This famous woodsman always went further into the wilderness than any other trapper, and his rounds of traps were spread over a larger area. He had to travel fifty miles through a trackless wilderness to make the circle of his traps. How true his Indian's instinct must have been to scatter several hundred traps over an area of fifty miles, and then go to them month after month unerringly. How easy one could have gone astray in the shifting gray glooms of the snow-laden forest, which changed from week to week as the snow was piled higher and higher and the full fury of winter settled on the land.

But Joe was never lost, and owing to his Indian inheritance, and his knowledge of the woods in wind and rain, snow and sleet, he rarely lost a trap.

He always located his cabin at a central point where he could return to it every two or three days.

His was not the ordinary shack but a well built cabin with a hole about six by eight under it called the cellar.

Why Joe wanted a good cabin, instead of a rude shack, and why he took pains to make it comfortable, you will see later.

On the fourth summer of his rambles, Shaggycoat went much

further from home than usual. This nomadic habit grew upon him, and each year he visited new lakes and streams. But this year he left all his old landmarks far behind and penetrated a new country.

Occasionally he saw signs that made him think this country was inhabited by the strange creature who had visited his lake two years before, in the great red duck. Something told him that it was a fearful country but curiosity and a desire to visit new places impelled him on and on.

Once he heard a loud pounding in the forest near the stream, and going cautiously forward, saw one of the strange creatures standing by a large tree, pounding upon it with mighty strokes. He was about to turn and flee from the place in haste, when he noticed a tremor in the top of the tree. He had seen this shudder in a tree many times before and knew well what it meant, so waited to watch and listen.

Then the strange creature struck upon the tree a few times more and it wavered, as though uncertain where to lay its tall form. Then with a rush and a roar, and a thunderous sound that rolled away through the forest, it fell and was no more a tree, but only a stick of timber.

When the sable mantle of night had been spread over the land and the creature who stood on his hind legs and pounded at the tree so vigorously had gone away, Shaggycoat went ashore and examined his work critically.

Tree-felling was in his line and this interested him very much.

Perhaps the queer creature was a beaver after all, for he was cutting trees just as they did about his own lake, but when he had examined the stump, he felt quite sure it was not the work of a beaver. The cleft was very smooth, and there were no teeth marks. The trunk had been cut in two, and here the cut was also smooth. The chips were much larger than those left by a beaver.

During the next few days Shaggycoat saw signs of much tree-cutting and they were all evidently cut by the creature who pounded on the trunk with his bright stick. The following week he came upon something that interested and astonished him even more than this, and that was a real dam, more symmetrical than his own, and holding in its strong arms a beautiful lake. He was sure that the dam was not made by beavers, for many of the logs used in its construction were too large for a beaver to manage. Besides there was a queer doorway in the middle of the dam for the water to run through. The lake was rather low and considerable water was escaping through the door.

Our industrious dam-builder thought this waste of water a great pity, and although the dam did not belong to him, he set to work and in half a day had stopped the sluiceway very effectively.

This industry greatly astonished the real owners of the dam, who discovered it a week later. They were a party of log-men, who had built the dam to help them in getting their logs through a long stretch of shallow water.

The following day Shaggycoat came upon a great number of logs in the stream.

They stretched miles and miles, and he thought these must be remarkable creatures, who could cut so many logs. He also thought it was getting to be a perilous country, and no place for a beaver who wished to live a long life, so he started homeward.

The leaves had just turned red upon the soft maple along the little water courses and that was a sign that he always heeded.

The second day of his return journey, while wading through a shallow in the stream, he put his remaining good forepaw in one of Joe Dubois's traps. It was only a mink trap, and would not have held, had he been given time to wrench himself free, but he had barely sprung the trap when the alder bushes on the bank parted and the celebrated trapper, club in hand, stood upon the shore within ten feet of the terrified beaver.

"Oh, by gar!" exclaimed Joe at the sight of him. "You is just one pig, fine skin by gar. I got you.

"Now you run away, I shoot. You keep still, I kill you with my club. That not tear you fine coat."

So Joe got hold of the end of the chain and began carefully working the beaver in toward him, holding the club ready.

When he had drawn poor Shaggycoat within striking distance he raised the club slowly.

The beaver saw the flash of the sunlight on the stick and the sinister look in Joe's eye, and something told him that his hour had come. He had seen a beaver killed once by a falling limb, and he knew quite well how stiff and motionless he would be when the club had descended. All in a second the picture of his woodland lake and Beaver City flashed before him and there was Brighteyes, and the beaver kids all waiting expectantly for him; all the colony waiting for his home-coming that they might begin repairs upon the dam.

The sun had never shone so brightly in all his life as it did at that moment, and the murmur of a brook had never sounded so sweet in his ears. But some great lady in the far away city was waiting impatiently for her cloak, and the factor at the post was holding out two bright shillings, so Joe brought the club down with a mighty stroke.

But the love of life was strong in Shaggycoat, as it is in nearly all animate things, so, quick as a flash, he twitched his head to one side, and the club fell in the stream with a great splash, filling the trapper's eyes with water.

"By gar," ejaculated Joe, blowing the water from his mouth, and laying down the club to wipe his eyes. "You is one mighty slick beaver, that you is, but it wasn't smart of you to get into my trap. Dat time you was one pig fool." Then a sudden inspiration came to Joe.

"By gar," he exclaimed, "I good mind to pring you home to my leetle gal. How she laugh when she see you. You pehave, I do it. You bother me, I prain you."

Then Joe scratched his head and thought. How could it be done? Finally a plan came to him, for he went to the alder bushes and cut a crotched stick, and another stick which was straight. With the crotched stick, he pinned Shaggycoat's neck to the ground, while with a piece of buckskin thong taken from his pocket he made a tight fitting collar for the beaver's neck. Then with another piece of thong he bound his hind legs tightly together. When this had been done, he passed a stout stick through the collar and the other end of it, between the beaver's hind legs. He then loosed the trap, and, grasping the stick half-way between the collar and the thong on the hind legs, started off with the unhappy beaver, carrying him, so that all the landscape looked upside down.

At first, Shaggycoat struggled violently but whenever he struggled Joe tapped him on the nose with his club and he soon saw that his best course was to keep still and let his captor carry him wherever he would.

The stick through the collar choked him so that he could hardly breathe, and the thong on his hind legs cut into the muscles, but even these discomforts were better than the club from which he had so narrowly escaped, so he behaved very well for a wild thing and watched Joe's every motion, always with a view of making a break for freedom at the first opportunity. But there seemed little chance of escape as long as the stick held him stretched out at his full length so that he could not get at his fetters.

So the woods went by with the trees all upside down, sticking their tops into the sky.

The blood surged into Shaggycoat's head, and his eyes grew dim. The great sleep was coming to him, that into which his grandfather had fallen, from which there was no awakening.

CHAPTER XIV

RUNNING-WATER

When Shaggycoat regained his sight and full consciousness, for the stick and the tight collar on his neck had choked him almost into the long sleep, he was lying on the floor of what seemed to be a very large lodge, only this lodge was square and his own in the beaver colony was circular. It was many times larger on the inside than even the great house in which Shaggycoat's own numerous family lived.

There must be some underground passages, he thought, just as there were in the beaver house, surely such powerful creatures as these would take that precaution. He would watch his chance, and before they knew it plunge down the tunnel to freedom.

Once in the water, this terrifying creature would not get hold of him again.

There were two of the strangers in the great lodge; the one with the cruel eyes, and a look that made Shaggycoat's long dark hair stand erect on his neck, and the other, smaller, and gentler.

When the smaller one talked, it was in a low, sweet voice that soothed Shaggycoat's wild terror of being held a prisoner.

Her voice reminded him of a little rill gurgling through pebbly grottoes, and he was glad when she spoke. When Shaggycoat first struggled to consciousness, she had been bending over him and somehow he was not afraid to have her look at him, for there was no murder in her eyes, as there was in Joe's.

"I pring him to you, leetle gal," said Joe, "one long way, by gar. He heavy, like one pig stone. He your beaver, you got no dog. He good pet when you tame him. Injun often keep tame beaver in lodge. He pretty, Wahawa, don't you think, leetle gal?"

"Yes, very handsome, Joe, and I thank you. He will make a good pet if I can tame him, but he is rather too old."

Wahawa, or Running-water, as her people called her, was Joe's Indian wife. She had been at the mission school for two years, and as she was very bright, spoke quite good English for the wilderness.

"See, how he trembles, Joe," she said. "He shakes like the aspen, when the fingers of the breezes are playing with it. Do you think I can tame him?"

"O yes, you tame anything," laughed Joe. "You tame me and I wild as hawk."

"See how he starts every time we move or speak," said the dusky daughter of the forest. "I am afraid we scare his wits out, before he knows us."

Shaggycoat squeezed into the darkest corner of the shack, where he stood trembling with fright. There were many sights and smells in the room that filled him with fear. First there was the strong repellent man-scent. This he always associated with traps and the "thunder stick" that killed the wild creatures so easily. One of these fearful things now rested on some hooks against the wall and the hooks looked very much like a deer's horns. There were a great many of those cruel things that lay in the water waiting for the paws of beaver or otter, hanging upon the wall, suspended by the rattling snake-like thing that Shaggycoat knew the sound of, as it clattered over the stones. Some of these things were also lying on the floor, and, as Joe kicked them into a corner, they made the noise that the beaver knew so well.

"Don't, Joe, you scare him," said the Indian girl, seeing how the beaver started at the sound.

"Py thunder, we not run this shack just for one beaver," retorted Joe. "He get used to noise. If he don't, I take his coat off, then he no mind noise."

At first the captive beaver was so terrified that he noticed almost nothing of his surroundings, but his eyes roamed wildly about for some underground passage through which he might escape, and, seeing none, he got as far into one corner as he could.

Presently he noticed what at first looked like another beaver lying on the floor asleep near him. But there was something strange and unnatural about the beaver that filled Shaggycoat with fear.

He seemed to be all flattened out just as though a tree or large stone had fallen upon him. But even any kind of a beaver's company was preferable to these creatures into whose power he had fallen, so Shaggycoat poked the sleeping beaver, to waken him.

His nose was not warm and moist, as it should have been, but dry and hard. Shaggycoat poked again, and the sleeping beaver moved, not by his own power, but the slight touch he had given had moved him. Again the bewildered Shaggycoat nosed his companion and the sleeper rolled over.

At the sight that met his eyes, every hair upon Shaggycoat's back and neck stood up, for the sleeping beaver was not a live beaver at all, but merely a beaver skin that had come off in some unaccountable manner. He had often seen the winter coat of the water-snake lying on the bank of the stream, but never that of a beaver. What strange unknown thing was this that had happened to his dead kinsman!

Presently Joe opened a trap-door in the floor to descend to his improvised cellar, and quick as a flash the captive beaver shot down ahead of him. But, alas, no fresh cool lake opened its inviting arms to receive him as he had expected. Instead of this he landed with a bump on the bottom of a cold, dark hole, which seemed even more like a prison than the room above.

It was something though to be away from their eyes, especially Joe's, and it was quiet down here and perhaps he could think what to do, so Shaggycoat wriggled into a far corner and kept very quiet while Joe rummaged about for flour and bacon. When he ascended the ladder to the room above, the beaver felt less terrified, although he knew that his plight was still desperate.

He had not been long alone when he began to dig himself a burrow in one corner of the cellar. Perhaps it would lead down to the lake, for surely these creatures would not be so foolish as to build their lodge on the land. Even if he could not strike water, the burrow would make a place of refuge where he could get away from the noise and the man-scent that fairly made his nostrils tingle.

So industriously he labored that when Wahawa came down the following morning to see if the beaver was spoiling their provisions, she could see nothing of him at first. Finally, after flashing the torchlight into all the corners, she discovered a pile of dirt, and holding the torch down to the entrance of the hole, found the beaver staring wild-eyed and pitifully up at her from the bottom of his new hiding-place.

"O thou, Puigagis, king of the beavers," she cried in a low rippling voice that again reminded the prisoner of the purling of a tiny stream, "come up to Wahawa, whose name is Running-water. She will not hurt you. She will feed you and caress you." The beaver was always the Indian's friend, teaching him industry and the need of a store of food for the cold winter months.

"Come up to Wahawa, O king of the beavers, and she will be your friend. The great trapper has gone to the lake and the streams to visit his many traps and cannot harm you; besides you belong to Running-water. Come up and she will be your friend."

But the poor captive only cowered at the bottom of his burrow and would not come up, so the Indian girl finally went away disappointed, but like the rest of her race she was patient, and knew that it takes days and weeks, or even months to gain the confidence of the wild creatures. Nevertheless she had accomplished more than she knew, for Shaggycoat was not afraid of her voice. There seemed something about its tones akin to the wind and the waters; a touch of nature, like the song of a bird or the murmur of distant rivers. There was something in the voice that told him this creature was kind.

Later on in the day when she brought him a maple sapling that she had cut with a hatchet, he felt that his confidence in the kindness of this stranger was not misplaced and although he was too frightened and homesick to eat, yet it did him good to see the tempting bark so near and to know that the Indian girl understood his wants.

When darkness again spread its sombre mantle over the land, Shaggycoat, hearing Joe's voice in the room above and the rattle of chains, as he kicked some traps into one corner, scurried into his burrow.

There were two events in Shaggycoat's life during the old days when he had been a beaver kid, playing with his brothers and sisters on the shores of their forest lake, in the old beaver city that he always remembered in time of peril. Both were startling and tragic and they had burned into his brain so deeply that he had never forgotten them, and he remembered them now in his lonely burrow.

One evening, just at twilight, he had been searching in the bushes along the shore for wild hops, a favorite dainty with young beavers, when he heard a noise in the woods close at hand. A strange noise always meant, "keep still and watch and listen." Although Shaggycoat was only five or six months old, the wild instinct of animal cunning was strong enough in him to prompt this wariness.

Presently the bushes parted and a tall, imperious creature came striding down to the lake. As he was coming directly for the spot where the young beaver was concealed, Shaggycoat made haste to scramble into the water, where he hid under the lily pads.

At the sound of his splashing, the tall creature stopped and snorted and stamped. He, too, was suspicious of strange noises, but, finally concluding that it was either a big bullfrog or a musquash, he strode down and began drinking in the lake. He stood very close to Shaggycoat, who should have kept quiet and let the stranger drink in peace, but curiosity, which is strong in many wild creatures, prompted the young beaver to peep out from under his lily pad screen at the tall stranger.

Shaggycoat did not think that the buck looked harmful so he slowly edged out from under the pads to get a better look at him. Then quick as a flash one of those slender hoofs rose and fell, and the young beaver went kicking to the bottom, leaving a bright streak of blood behind him. One of the older beavers found him half an hour later, lying on his back in the lily pads, stunned and bleeding. His head did not resume its normal size for several days, but the event taught him a lesson that he never forgot and after that day curiosity was always tempered with prudence.

The second event that Shaggycoat could never forget happened like the first just at dusk. This time neither he nor his brother with whom he was playing was at fault, but the thing happened, as things do in the woods and the waters, and when the ripple had passed, the lake was as placid and smiling as ever.

They were playing in the shallows. The game might have been water-tag, or perhaps it was just rough and tumble, but, in either event, they were having a jolly time. The sun had just set in a blaze of glory at the upper end of the lake and long shadows were stealing across the water. Then upon the stillness there broke a peculiar sound, who-o-o, who-o-o, who-o-o, who-o-o; the first few notes long and loud, and the last short and soft like an echo. It was the hunting cry of the great horned owl, going forth on his twilight quest for food. There were two impatient owlets in the top of a tall tree, back in the woods who were waiting for their supper of mice and chipmunks or small birds. But Shaggycoat and his brother had never even heard of the great horned owl so they continued their romp in the lily pads.

Who-o-o, who-o-o, who-o-o, who-o-o, came the cry again, this time close at hand, but the young beavers continued their play and the great horned owl his hunt.

Suddenly Shaggycoat noticed something large above them that darkened the sky and which kept flapping like the bushes along the lake when the wind blew. There were two fiery, yellow balls and a strong hook between them, and two other sets of hooks that looked sharp as the brambles on the thorn-bush. This much Shaggycoat saw, for the great flapping thing was just above them and much nearer than he wished. Then a set of hooks reached down and gripped his brother in the back of the neck and bore him away. Higher and higher the strange thing went, carrying the owlets' supper in the strong set of hooks, and Shaggycoat knew by the piteous cry floating back that something dreadful had happened, but he was too young to understand just what.

Then a strange terror of the woods and the shore came over him and he fled to the lodge and did not leave it again for days.

Where his brother went, and who the stranger was, Shaggycoat never knew, but the owlets in the top of the tall tree in the deep woods tasted beaver meat and found it good.

CHAPTER XV

KING OF BEAVERS

"Joe," said Wahawa to the trapper one evening, as they sat by the fire, munching corn bread and bacon, "I believe you have caught the sacred beaver of my people, the good Puigagis, King of all the Beavers."

Joe laughed. "Py gar, what foolishness you tink in your hade now. You is one foolish leetle gal, he your sacred beaver, you say?"

But Wahawa did not laugh. She looked very serious as she replied, "It is nothing to laugh at, Joe. If this is really the sacred beaver, no good will come of it. Did you notice he had lost one forepaw? My people always let a maimed beaver go when they trap him because of something that happened many moons ago. Listen, Joe, and I will tell."

The man of many traps looked interested for he, too, was touched with superstition, and fearful of anything that might affect his good luck as a trapper.

"As many moons ago as the old pine back of the shack has needles on its boughs," began Wahawa, "the Great Spirit became angry with my people. The squaws said it was because the warriors went on the war-path instead of killing and preparing meat for the winter months, and the braves said it was because the squaws were lazy and did not raise corn. But for one reason or another the Manito was angry so he covered the face of the sun with his right hand, and it was like a sick man's smile, and he covered the moon and the stars by night with his blanket and they were no longer bright, but like a camp-fire that has gone out.

"The corn did not grow in the summer-time, and the snow and the wind were furious in the winter.

"Such cold as this was never known in the land before and never since. The ice froze so deeply on lake and river that it could not be broken and no fish could be taken. The deer all yarded in the deep forest and did not stir abroad so the hunters could not find them, and many perished before spring. Still deeper and deeper fell the snow and colder and colder grew the breath of the wind, and the kiss of the frost was like death.

"The warm skins of bear and beaver were no longer warm and the camp-fire had lost its heat.

"Finally, the warriors were obliged to kill their ponies, and the wolves, running in great packs, came down to help with the feast. At night they would stand about the camp, just on the border of the firelight, watching and waiting. They seemed to know that powder and ball were low in the pouch of the warrior, and that he no longer had strength to draw the bow. They knew that the camp-fires would soon go out, and the warriors and the squaws fall asleep at their post. So the great gray wolfs watched and waited for they knew that the hour of feasting was near at hand.

"Then my grandmother, who was the daughter of the chief, and whose withered lips told me the story, had a dream.

"She dreamed that Puigagis, the King of the Beavers, came into her lodge and spoke to her in the tongue of her people.

"'O Singing Bird, daughter of the great chief,' he said, and his voice was sweet to hear. 'The great spirit was angry because his warriors did not hunt, and the women were lazy, but he has seen the suffering of thy people, and the great wolf, Famine, looking in at your lodges. This melted his anger and he has sent me to save your people. Tell your father, the chief, to send his warriors in the morning to a valley, one day's march to the northward, and they shall find a colony of beavers as large as an Indian village. Many lodges they shall see, and all will contain beaver meat, and warm furs to protect them and their women against the wind and frost. I, Puigagis, the King of all the Beavers, will go before them to show the way. My own life and all the lives of my kind I will give to save the lives of the redmen and their daughters.'

"Then the wind lifted Puigagis, King of the Beavers, in its strong arms and bore him away over the tree-tops.

"The daughter of the chief awoke and saw that the camp-fire was very low, and that the wind was shaking the tepee as though to tear it down. When she put new faggots on the fire and it blazed up, she saw there were beaver tracks on the snow and her dream had been true. She awoke her father, the chief, who called his warriors and they examined the tracks in the snow and saw that they were the tracks of a beaver; a beaver of great size, who had lost one forepaw in a trap.

"The chief then bade his warriors make ready for in the morning they would go to the lake of which the King of the Beavers had spoken.

"In the morning the sun was brighter than it had been for weeks, and they started out with more hope than they had felt for many moons. They went due north as Puigagis, the King of the Beavers, had directed, and, whenever they were uncertain of the way, they would examine the snow and always at just the right moment would find the tracks of the three-footed beaver.

"Although he went on the wings of the wind, he touched the snow every mile or two that they might not go astray and miss the Beaver Lake.

"Late in the afternoon, when they were weary and very cold with the long march, they came to a beautiful valley, and there before them, covered with snow, stretched the broad bosom of the lake.

"Here and there showing their domes above the ice were beaver lodges, many more than the oldest hunters had ever seen. On the top of the largest lodge of all sat Puigagis, King of all the Beavers, and the warriors saw that his right forepaw had been taken off by a trap. A moment he sat there as though in welcome, then disappeared as if the lodge had opened and swallowed him.

"Then the warriors built great fires upon the ice, made a hole in the beaver dam with their hatchets and strong stakes which they cut in the woods, and destroyed the entire colony, with the exception of the great lodge of Puigagis, King of all the Beavers. This they would not touch, lest evil befall them; nor will they take the skin of a maimed beaver to this day.

"They loaded their packs with meat and skins until they bent beneath them. The wind and weather befriended them on their homeward journey. The beaver meat and the new skins kept life in the Indian village until the great Spirit lifted his hand from the face of the sun, till flowers and birds returned and the children of the woods were again glad.

"But the three-footed beaver they will not trap or harm to this day and it is an ill omen to hold one captive."

"Dat ees vun fine story," commented Joe, as the narrator finished. "Maybe he true, maybe he not. I do not know me. But he ver good," and Joe blew rings of blue smoke and watched them meditatively.

"Did you ever hear how the beaver got his flat tail?" asked Wahawa.

"By gar, no, I tink he always have he. Tell one more pretty story, leetle gal."

"Well, this was the way," replied the Indian girl.

"Many, many moons ago, so long ago that it is only known by

pictures that my people cut in stone, there was a King Beaver, wiser and larger than all his fellows. In those days, the beaver had a round bushy tail like the raccoon, but he saw one day when he was building a house that it would be very handy to have a flat tail. He pondered long on how to get it. Finally a plan came to him and he called the four strongest beavers in the land and told them to bring a large flat stone.

"When they had brought the stone, the King Beaver placed his tail upon another flat stone and made the four strong beavers drop the stone they had brought upon his tail. It hurt him very much but he shut his teeth tight and thought how nice it would be to have a flat tail. When they lifted the stone off his tail, it was not as flat as he wished, so they tried again, but still it did not suit him, but he thought they had flattened it enough for that day.

"Every day for a week he had the four strong beavers drop the stone on his tail until at last it was flat enough. After that he used it so much in handling mud that the hair soon wore off, and it looked just as the beaver tail does now. The descendants of this beaver all had flat tails, and they were so much stronger and better workmen that they survived all the other kinds and the round-tailed beavers soon became extinct.

"There is another Indian legend about how the beaver learned to build houses. Once an Indian caught a beaver in a pitfall and took him home to his wigwam where he kept him all winter. The beaver saw how warm and nice the Indian house was and the following fall when he escaped he built himself a mud house as near like the Indian's as he could, and he was the first beaver to live in a lodge."

"Ver good stories," commented Joe. "Ver good. Maybe they true, maybe they not, but I tink He make um beaver tail flat, because He know the beaver want a flat tail. And for He," Joe pointed with his thumb to the roof of the shack, "He give de eagle hees strong wing because he live in the cloud, an' de fish fins, because he want to swim. He made de deer with springs in his laigs because he got no teeth to bite his enemy, nor claws. He made de fox cunning becase he not strong, so he run mighty fast like de wind. De wildcat an' de bar, He also give claws an' strong arms, so they all lib an' not starb.

"De flower it smile, an' de tree talk an' de wind an' de water they better company than much folks. Dar no lie in de woods. Dar all tings good. He make all tings ver good, by gar. Me like um wind an' water. They all make me glad."

One day when Shaggycoat had been in captivity about a week, Wahawa came down to his burrow and coaxed and dragged him out. He was not so much afraid of her as he had been and he loved the sound of her voice, for it was like the water slipping between stones. But when she had brought him forth, Wahawa did something that both astonished and frightened the beaver, for, quick as a flash, she threw a camp blanket over his head, and before he had time to bite, she had gathered up the four corners and Shaggycoat was a prisoner in an improvised bag.

Although he bit and clawed at the blanket, it was so soft and yielding that he could make no impression on it, so he finally lay still and let the Indian girl do with him what she would. She talked to him all the time in that low rippling voice which somewhat allayed his fear.

She slowly ascended the ladder leading to the room above with the heavy load upon her back and then rested him for a moment on the floor.

What new peril awaited him, Shaggycoat did not know. Maybe his coat was to be taken off now, and he would be just like the poor beaver he had seen the first night of his captivity. But Wahawa soon lifted him to her strong back again and bore him away, he knew not where. When she had carried him about a quarter of a mile over rough country, she laid down her burden, and, to the great astonishment of the beaver, dropped the four corners of the blanket and the beautiful world that Shaggycoat had known before his captivity, the world with a sky and fresh green trees and bushes with grass and sweet smelling air, was before him. But better than all that a swift stream was flowing almost at his very feet. The music of its rippling made him wild with joy.

Here was freedom almost within reach. But his captor was standing by and the buckskin collar was still about his neck and he imagined it held him in some mysterious manner. He looked up at the Indian girl with large pleading eyes, and she understood his misgivings, so she drew the hunting knife from her belt and severed the buckskin collar. It had cut into his neck for so long that the beaver did not realize it was gone until he saw it lying on the ground, then his heart gave a great bound. Was freedom to be his after all? His nostrils dilated as he looked furtively about. There was his captive standing by him and her eyes were full of kindness. There was the water calling to him, calling as it had never called before, but he did not quite know what it all meant. Then the Indian girl spoke and he understood.

"Go, Puigagis, King of the Beavers," she said. "Go and be happy after thy kind. We have held thee captive too long. Go at once, lest evil befall us."

With a sudden jump, a scramble and a great splash, Shaggycoat clove the water of the deep pool at their feet. The ripples widened and widened and a few bubbles rose to the surface as the dark form sank from sight and Puigagis disappeared as suddenly from the life of the Indian girl as though the earth had opened and swallowed him.

Once she thought she saw a dark form gliding stealthily along under the shadow of the further bank, but was not sure. Although she watched and listened for a long time, she saw or heard nothing of him. Puigagis, King of the Beavers, had gone to his kind. The lakes and the streams had reclaimed their wilderness child, and the Indian girl was glad.

CHAPTER XVI

OLD SHAG

Eight years have now passed since Shaggycoat brought his mate into the beautiful wilderness valley, and they had proceeded to make it habitable, according to the ideas of a beaver.

Wonderful changes have taken place in the alder meadow since then, and one would not know it to be the same spot. It is no more an alder meadow, but a beautiful forest lake stretching away into the distance until it is lost between the foothills, nearly two miles above the dam. On either side, the sparkling waters flow back to the amphitheatre of hills that enfold it and the lake is altogether like a wonderful sparkling jewel set in the emerald surrounding of the foothills.

Each summer, during his wanderings, Shaggycoat has met other wanderers like himself, and many of them have returned with him to his mountain lake. Even the first autumn, when he returned with his amputated paw, a pair of sleek beavers came with him, so there were two beaver lodges in the pond during the second winter instead of one. The dam was also strengthened and broadened during that second autumn until the pond was twice its original size.

The third spring Shaggycoat's own first family of beavers left the lodge to roam during the summer months, and to return in the autumn with mates. This is the arrangement in a well ordered beaver lodge. The children stay with their parents until they are three years of age, so a lodge usually contains the babies, the yearlings and two-year-olds, who allow themselves shelter under the family lodge until their third birthday, when they are shoved out to make room for the babies who have just come. So there is a general nose breaking at this time, and the elders are sent into the world while all the rest are promoted. But I do not imagine that they have to be shoved very hard, for their love of freedom and wild life, and also the mating instinct, is calling to them that third year, and they always obey the call of nature.

It must not be imagined that the little dam originally built on the spot, flows all this broad expanse of country, for, as we have already seen, year by year it has been added to, until now the gorge is blocked by a log and stone structure that would do credit to man, with all his building and engineering skill. It seems to me that the beaver, with his building instinct, and his ingenuity in making his world over to suit his manner of life, more nearly resembles man than any other wild creature.

Each beaver colony is a veritable city, and each lodge contains a large and well ordered family.

The house is always scrupulously clean, and each member of the family has his own bed which he occupies. The front gate is surrounded by a moat, like the castles of old, and the drawbridge is always up.

The beaver is a veritable Venitian, and his city is a real Venice, with its waterway and its islands of solid earth upon which stand the houses of its many citizens. The new dam which is most important to Beaver City, for it holds the water above the entrances of the score or more of houses, is a fine structure about two hundred feet in length, and nine feet in diameter at its base. Into the structure many thousand logs have been rolled, some of them coming from two or three miles up the lake, for timber is not so plentiful near to the dam as it was.

The engineering genius of this huge undertaking was Shaggycoat, who sat upon his broad flat tail and directed his many workmen. Near by, seated upon the top of one of the lodges, a sentinel was always posted while they worked. He warned them of danger, and they gave their whole attention to the work. At the first suspicious sound he would bring his broad tail down upon the water with a resounding slap that could be heard all along the dam, and all through Beaver City, for water is very mobile, and conducts motion or sound easily. At this well-known signal, the workers who, a moment before, might have been lifting and tugging logs or laying on mortar, would disappear as though the lake had opened and swallowed them. This was really just what happened, but the waters did not open; they were always waiting and ready to receive their little water folks.

For a few moments the lake would be as quiet as though there were not a beaver in the whole shimmering expanse, then a brown muzzle, dripping water, would be cautiously thrust up from some shady corner of the dam, and a careful reconnaissance made. When the beaver had made sure that it was a false alarm, he would call the rest and work would go on as before.

Most of the conical shaped houses, of which there are now about twenty, are on islands or on the bank near the dam. They look as much like a small Indian village, as they do like the abodes of wild animals.

For a long time, the overflow water from the lake troubled the beavers by wearing away their dam, but, finally, they dug a little channel in the sand around one end of the dam, and now the water runs off nicely in this artificial duct, and the dam is left unimpaired by the flow. If you could stand upon this dam, partly overgrown by willows, and see the symmetrical structure and the little lodges of Beaver City above, and the sparkling water running nicely away in the sluiceway, you would marvel at the ingenuity and patience of these ingenious rodents. But the wisest and oldest head in the colony is that of Shaggycoat, or old Shag, as I shall now call him, for he was the pioneer of the city, and his was the first lodge on the large island.

Little by little he has seen his lake widen and broaden, and one by one new lodges have been reared, until now, as he sits upon his broad tail and views Beaver City from the vantage ground of the dam, he must be well satisfied with his planning, for it is all his world and he loves it as each wild creature does the element it inhabits. To his ears the sound of running water is sweetest music, and the roar of the freshet, which fills man with dismay has no terrors for him; he knows it is only his beloved water world, wild and turbulent, with the joy of melting snow, and the bliss of spring rains.

He also knows that soon the buds will start and the birds sing, and he will be off for his summer ramble. He has never outgrown the habit of wandering during the summer months, but autumn will surely see him back directing repairs upon the dam and seeing that the winter supply of unpeeled logs is stored. It takes a great many logs to supply Beaver City with food now so that when the winter supply is piled up in the water in front of the dam, it would probably make several cords. If you could have seen the everchanging beauty of that forest lake through spring, summer, autumn and winter, you would not have been surprised that the beavers were well satisfied with their surroundings, or that the water seemed always to be calling to them in low sweet tones.

When the spring freshet filled their lake to overflowing, the ice piled up against the dam, and the mad waters rushed through the crevasse roaring and hissing like an infuriated monster. Though the waters were angry and tossed the great cakes of ice about disdainfully, yet the foam upon its fretful surface looked soft as wool and the little water folks knew that the anger would pass, even as the fury of the spring wind.

Finally the water would go down, and the lake would become clear and calm. Then it was a wonderful opal like the spring sky from which it took its color. When the warm spring winds kissed its sparkling surface, it dimpled and sparkled, and little wavelets lapped the pebbly beach with a low soft sound.

Then June came with its lily pads, and the pickerel grass in the shallows along the edge, and the waters near shore were green like emerald. July brought the lilies, whose mysterious sweetness ravished the nostrils, and whose creamy white faces nestled among the green pads in sweet content.

The summer passed like a wonderful dream with soft skies, balmy winds, and warm delightful waters in which to swim, but the male beavers over three years of age were always away during the summer, and the lake was left to the females and the youngsters.

Soon autumn came and the maples back in the foothills were made gorgeous by the first frost. The merry fall winds soon rattled down showers of scarlet, crimson, yellow and golden leaves till the waters along the edge of the lake were as bright as the branches above. Even then the trees were all reflected in the lake, so it had its own beauty as well as that of the world above it.

When the first frost came, the male beavers returned to repair the dam, and build new lodges or repair the old ones. These were active nights when the sky was so thick with stars that there was hardly room for more, and the Milky Way was bright and luminous.

When the clear glass window was shut down over the lake and the beavers in their snug city were made prisoners for the winter, December had come.

Then the whole lake sparkled like a jewel, and by night it vied with the stars for mysterious beauty; but soon the lake would be covered with snow, and then it would be a wonderful marble floor, smooth as a board stretching away as far as the eye could reach.

There snugly locked under the ice, where not even the gluttonous wolverine can dig them out, with plenty of food for the coming winter, let us leave the inhabitants of Beaver City, happy in the assurance that spring will come again when their lake will be warm and bright, nestling like a wonderful jewel on the breast of mother earth.

* * * * *

www.ingramcontent.com/pod-product-compliance
Lightning Source LLC
Chambersburg PA
CBHW070119290526
45789CB00005B/2072